ROLLS-ROYCE & BENTLEY

The history of the cars

WHATEVER IS RIGHTLY DONE,
HOWEVER HUMBLE, IS NOBLE.
Royce, 1924

THE BEST CAR IN THE WORLD

ROLLS-ROYCE & BENTLEY

The history of the cars

MARTIN BENNETT

First published in 1996

British Library Cataloguing-in-Publication Data:
A catalogue record for this book is available from the British Library

ISBN 0 85429 972 6

Library of Congress catalog card No. 96-075167

G. T. Foulis & Company is an imprint of Haynes Publishing, Sparkford, Nr Yeovil, Somerset, BA22 7JJ

Typeset by J. H. Haynes & Co. Ltd

Printed in Great Britain

As part of our ongoing market research, we are always pleased to receive comments about our books, suggestions for new titles, or requests for catalogues. Please write to: The Editorial Director, G. T. Foulis & Co., Sparkford, Nr Yeovil, Somerset, BA22 7JJ.

Contents

Introduction

When the original edition of *Rolls-Royce: The History of the Car* was first published in 1973 there were few general books on Rolls-Royce and Bentley cars and none that were completely up to date. The books that were available either dealt with specialised aspects of the cars or were quite expensive, or both. *Rolls-Royce: The History of the Car* was intended to provide the enthusiast with a basic history of the development of the cars in an attractive 'coffee table'-type package at a price that anyone could afford. Most of the illustrations were either previously unpublished or had not been published for many years.

Nowadays, more than 20 years later, all that has changed. Books on the Rolls-Royce and Bentley marques, from the superb and scholarly to the good and indifferent, have proliferated. *Rolls-Royce: The History of the Car* has long since begun to look decidedly inadequate and dated both in its design and content. Whilst I have since turned my attention to other projects, the opportunity to completely revise the book was extremely attractive, and what was intended to be a Third Edition became *Rolls-Royce & Bentley: the History of the Cars* – an acknowledgement that this is in fact an entirely new book which is as completely up to date as a rapidly changing world allows. Its purpose, however, remains unchanged: to provide a basic overview of Rolls-Royce (and post-1933 Bentley) motor car history.

The reasons for buying an older Rolls-Royce or Bentley car rather than a new lesser make are equally as valid now as when I wrote the original 1973 Introduction. However, Mk VI Bentleys can no longer be purchased 'for a few hundred pounds', and the Silver Shadow, the current model in 1973, has become the 'entry level' model for many people entering the Rolls-Royce and Bentley hobby today. And a hobby of many exponents it has become over the past couple of decades. The Rolls-Royce Enthusiasts' Club, based in the UK, now boasts more than 8,500 members in an impressive number of countries; the Rolls-Royce Owners' Club in America can claim around 7,000, while the Rolls-Royce Owners' Club of Australia adds a further thousand or so to the total and there are smaller clubs in other countries.

Martin Bennett
Goulburn, New South Wales, 1996

Acknowledgements

The vast majority of the illustrations in this book (most of those not listed below) have been provided over many years by Rolls-Royce Motor Cars Ltd, many being provided specifically for this new book, and author and publisher record their sincere appreciation of the Company for so much generous co-operation.

Other invaluable contributions were made by Klaus-Josef Roßfeldt, whose generosity in supplying his superb photographs to meet particular requirements is very much appreciated, and by Tom Clarke, whose unrivalled knowledge of the Royce and very early Rolls-Royce cars was drawn upon to ensure that the early history of the cars are recorded here is as accurate as possible. Steve Stuckey, a recognised expert on the Phantom III, rose to the occasion when photographs of that model were required. Thanks are also due to Richard Mann, a Quality Engineer at the former Mulliner Park Ward, Hythe Road coachbuilding works, for sharing his wealth of practical and anecdotal knowledge of post-war coachbuilding.

This is the third title to include some of the superb drawings of talented artist John Bull, and his contribution to this book is gratefully acknowledged.

Thanks are recorded to the following for providing illustrations as indicated:

The Autocar – 32, 42, 58 (top), 82 (top), 76 (bottom), Doug Bristow – dust jacket (front, lower), 126 (top); John Bull – 12 (bottom), 27 (top), 62 (bottom), 96 (bottom), 131 (centre); Jack Barclay Ltd – 61 (centre), 62 (second from top), 63 (bottom), 64 (bottom left & bottom right), 98 (top & centre), 100 (bottom), 101 (bottom), 107 (bottom), 110 (bottom), 116 (top & centre), 117 (top), 102 (lower); Canberra Historical Society – 28; Graham Cornish – 22 (bottom), 65 (bottom); Jim Kelso – dust jacket (front, top), 69 (lower); David Scott-Montcrieff – 62 (top); Lord Montagu of Beaulieu – 26 (top); Roger Morrison – 66 (lower); *The Motor* – 34; Klaus-Josef Roßfeldt – dust jacket (rear, top), 26 (bottom), 36 (bottom) 37, 38, 40 (top), 65 (top), 67 (top), 72 (top), 76 (top), 124 (top); Tom Solley – 50 (centre & bottom), 84 (bottom); Carl Stockton – 66 (top).

Chapter One

Establishing the tradition

'Ninety Years of Motor Car Excellence' is one way of encapsulating the nine decades since Frederick Henry Royce's first two-cylinder motor car was first driven so unobtrusively on to the streets of Manchester. The story of the meeting of and subsequent partnership between the intuitive mechanic Royce and the aristocratic motorist and businessman The Hon Charles Stewart Rolls is one that has

been told and re-told many times. No new facts are claimed for this version, which closely follows the 'official' story.

Charles Stewart Rolls was born in 1877, the third son of Lord and Lady Llangattock of The Hendre, an extensive estate in Monmouthshire. The young Rolls was sent to Eton where he shunned the usual sports in favour of dabbling in science, though he demonstrated outstanding skill as a

Charles Stewart Rolls (1877-1910). Rolls was a born adventurer who took up cycle racing, motor racing, ballooning and powered flying in turn, and was a pioneer motorist and aviator in England. He attended the World's Car Rally in Paris in 1894 – two years before horseless carriages were even allowed on British roads! In 1903 he started his business, C. S. Rolls & Co, dealing in motor cars, a little later acquiring premises in Conduit Street, which subsequently became the London offices of Rolls-Royce Ltd. Before his untimely death in a flying accident in Bournemouth in 1910, at the age of 33, Rolls had distinguished himself by such feats as the first double crossing of the English Channel.

cyclist. He installed electricity at The Hendre at a time when such a modern convenience was by no means the norm.

On a visit to France with his father in 1894 it came forcefully to his attention that the motor car was developing in that country at a speed that was rendered impossible in England by the 'Red Flag Act' and other absurdities imposed by a Parliament dominated by a horse-loving gentry. While in France the 17-year-old Rolls acquired a small French motor car – a Peugeot. A few months after bringing the car to England he used it to drive from the family town house in London to University at Cambridge, where he was studying engineering.

One can only imagine what a gruelling journey this must have been on the appalling roads of the time, at an average speed of 4½ miles per hour. However, even that derisory speed represented a road speed record for the distance, and given the then speed limit of 4 miles per hour meant that he had broken the law throughout much of the journey! As an indication of how ambitious such a journey by road was regarded in those days, it is worth mentioning that Rolls saw fit to give prior notification to the Chief Constables of Hertfordshire and Cambridgeshire of his planned route. The car was a typical horseless carriage of the period, with tiller steering, a German (Daimler) 3¾ hp engine under the seats, chain drive and wire wheels more akin to those of a bicycle than a motor car.

At Christmas, Rolls drove the car home to Monmouthshire, a distance of 140 miles, which took two days – a journey that he could have completed in a few hours by train. It was the first time a motor car of any kind had been seen in or around Monmouth.

In 1896 the road speed limit was raised to 12 miles per hour. Rolls's next car was a 12 hp Panhard – a much faster and more powerful machine than the Peugeot and, though still chain-driven, possessed of a proper bonnet and steering wheel. In 1900 he won the first Thousand Miles Reliability Trial, promoted by Lord Northcliffe and the Automobile Club of Great Britain and Northern Ireland, of which Rolls was a Founder Member and which later became the RAC.

In Edwardian England the choice of 'respectable' occupations for a man of Rolls's class was extremely limited. Rolls, however, was not a man to be hobbled by convention, and in 1903, with a degree in Mechanics and Applied Science and the letters MIME after his name, he saw no social impediment to setting up as a motor car importer and dealer, with workshops at Lillie Hall, Fulham, and showrooms and offices in Brook Street, Mayfair, later moving to Conduit Street.

Unlike the aristocratic Rolls, Frederick Henry Royce came from much more lowly beginnings. He was born in 1863 at Alwalton in Cambridgeshire*, the son of a miller. It seems that Royce's family was not prosperous, because in 1877 the family moved to London, apparently abandoning the mill, and at ten years of age Royce was working as a newspaper boy for W. H. Smith at London railway stations, notably Clapham Junction, to help support his family. His father had died the previous year.

At 14 Royce was apprenticed to the Great Northern Railway at the company's Peterborough workshops, a change in fortunes brought about by a kindly aunt who paid the £20 per year premium and for his board and lodging. The strict railway workshop regime, together with his natural intuition and aptitude, provided the basis for the skills that were to become legendary.

After three years the generous aunt was no longer able to keep up the payments and the 17-year-old Royce found himself, in the depths of a depression, looking for employment. After working 16-hour days for a machine tool company in Leeds he

The statue of Charles Rolls in his native Monmouth.

Other authors have placed Alwalton variously in Lincolnshire, Northamptonshire and even Rutland! However, Royce himself gave Huntingdonshire as the county of his birth. The village of Alwalton now falls within the present-day boundaries of Cambridgeshire.

Frederick Henry Royce (1863-1933, later Sir Henry Royce, Bart) at the age of 33.

was fortunate enough to obtain a job as a tester with a pioneer electric light and power company in London. He studied the then relatively new science of electricity at night, and at the age of 19 was sent to Liverpool as a technical expert for the Lancashire Maxim and Western Electric Company.

Two years later, with £70 capital – £20 of his own and £50 from his friend A. E. Claremont – Royce started his business, F. H. Royce & Co, in Cooke Street, Hulme, Manchester, with Claremont as his partner, making electric light fittings and, later, domestic electric bell sets. In 1894 the firm graduated to the manufacture of electric motors, dynamos and switch-gear, and became Royce Ltd. Soon after began the manufacture of the Royce electric crane, of which large numbers were used in docks, railway yards, factories and mines all over Britain and other parts of the world. Royce was a successful businessman, had married and built a fine house, but years of long hours, overwork and poor eating habits were already beginning to take their toll.

In 1903 Royce bought a motor car – a second-hand Decauville – for

Royce in the 1920s by the garden gate at 'Elmstead', his country home at West Wittering on the Sussex coast. From here he and his design team carried out both motor car and aero design work.

commuting between the factory at Hulme (and also now at Trafford Park) and his home at Knutsford, 15 miles each way. He was immediately impatient with its difficult starting, temperamental ignition system, overheating and noise, and decided that he could build a better motor car himself. Much to his partner Claremont's irritation, Royce announced that a batch of three two-cylinder motor cars would be built at Cooke Street as a precursor to planned larger-scale motor car production.

History records that the first complete 10 hp Royce car was driven out of the Cooke Street, Manchester,

works of Royce Ltd by Henry Royce himself on 1 April 1904. For fairly obvious reasons, the date of the first run was recorded as 31 March. The car was driven to Royce's home in Knutsford, about 15 miles distant.

The engine of this charming little creation had two cylinders of 3¾ inch bore and 5 inch stroke, and was said to have developed about 12 bhp at 1,000 rpm. The valve layout was overhead inlet and side exhaust ('F'-head), a layout that was to appear again 42 years later on the Silver Wraith and Bentley Mk VI. The drive from the engine was transmitted to the three-speed gearbox via a leather-lined cone-type clutch and a universal

The chassis of the first Royce car, photographed at the back of the Cooke Street works. It was this car that Royce drove on 1 April 1904 to his home in Knutsford, 15 miles away.

joint. The footbrake operated on the drive-shaft and the handbrake on the rear wheels.

The freedom from noise and vibration achieved by Royce, as well as the ability to throttle down to a quiet tick-over, broke new ground for a two-cylinder car, and set the standard for the cars that were later to bear the name Rolls-Royce.

The second Royce car became the property of Royce's partner, A. E. Claremont, and the third was used by Royce himself after the first car was handed over to C. S. Rolls for his use as a London demonstrator.

Claremont was also a director of the Trafford Park Power & Light Company and of W. T. Glover & Co Ltd, and it was Henry Edmunds of

Although no Royce cars as such survive, the engine of the second Royce car, chassis 15881, is preserved in Manchester. It is seen here with, from left to right, Dr F. Llewellyn Smith, the first post-war Managing Director of Rolls-Royce Ltd, Motor Car Division; Fred Bates; and J. O. H. Norris, Managing Director, Cockshoot & Co, Manchester.

Glover's who first arranged for Royce and the Hon C. S. Rolls to meet. Edmunds was a pioneer motorist, a founder of the Automobile Club of Great Britain and Ireland, an inventor and a friend of Charles Rolls. On 26 March 1904 Edmunds wrote to Royce Ltd as follows:

'I saw Mr Rolls yesterday, after telephoning to you; and he said it would be much more convenient if you could see him in London, as he is so very much occupied; and, further, that several other houses are now in negotiation with him, wishing to do the whole or part of his work. What he is looking for is a good high-class quality car to replace the Panhard; preferably of three or four cylinders. He has some personal dislike of two-cylinder cars. I will do all I can to bring about this arrangement with Mr Rolls; for I think your car deserves well; and ought to take its place when it is once recognised by the public on its merits.'

This letter confirmed that Rolls was suspicious of two-cylinder cars and that he was at first unenthusiastic about travelling all the way to Manchester to see Royce's. Edmunds then wrote to Rolls as follows:

'I have pleasure in enclosing you photographs and specification of the Royce car, which I think you will agree with me looks very promising. I have written them asking if they can make an early appointment to meet you in London and also whether they can arrange to send up a car for your inspection and trial. The point that impressed me most, however, was this. The people have worked out their design in their own office, and knowing as I do, the skill of Mr Royce as a practical mechanical engineer, I feel one is very safe in taking up any work his firm may produce.'

Rolls's reluctance to travel to Manchester was balanced by his patriotic desire to market a high-quality British motor car rather than having to import them from the Continent. It is even possible that he had already seen the first Royce car at the Sideslip Trials in London.

On 29 April 1904 Rolls wrote to Edmunds to ask him if he could

Two views of the third Royce car, showing the shape of the Royce radiator. This was the longest surviving of the three Royces, being used as a mail hack, in which guise it is seen here, at the Derby works of Rolls-Royce Ltd until well into the 1920s.

'come up to Manchester any time next week'. Edmunds recalled that in the dining car of the train travelling to Manchester for the first meeting with Royce, Rolls had remarked that it was his ambition that his name should be associated with a motor car, the name of which would become a household word, just as Steinway with pianos, Chubb with safes, etc. To what extent his ambition was soon to be realised he could scarcely have imagined; the name 'Rolls-Royce' was soon to become synonymous with the best that money could buy, and passed into the language as a byword for excellence, people still unconsciously using it to infer that something is the best obtainable.

Rolls was suitably impressed by Royce and the quality of his products, and soon after their meeting in May 1904, Rolls the London car dealer and Royce the Manchester engineer reached an agreement that C. S. Rolls & Co would sell the entire motor car output of Royce Ltd. Soon after, it was agreed that the cars should be called 'Rolls-Royce'. A formal agreement to that effect was signed on 23 December 1904.

After Rolls had agreed to sell all the motor cars that Royce could produce, the little 10 hp remained in production, though now with the name Rolls-Royce. The rather nondescript radiator shape of the Royce cars gave way, on all but the first two 10 hp Rolls-Royce cars, to a distinctive radiator, which, in one form or another but always readily recognisable, has graced every* Rolls-Royce car to this day. The retention of the Royce radiator shape for the first two Rolls-Royce 10 hp cars probably explains the recollections of at least one former Royce employee, decades later, that there were five Royce cars rather than the three that history records.

The first badge to appear on the Rolls-Royce radiator was oval in shape. A little later the famous rectangular 'R-R' monogram was designed, but by whom seems not to have been recorded and remains open to speculation.

* Occasionally a coachbuilder has omitted or shrouded the Rolls-Royce radiator or its outer shell.

For many years, because of its radiator shape, this was believed to be a picture of one of the three Royce cars. However, it is now known that the first two Rolls-Royce cars built had the Royce radiator, the third Rolls-Royce being the first to have the distinctive new radiator. The car in this picture is now believed to be the first Rolls-Royce car, 10 hp chassis 20150.

After the initial two chassis, all subsequent 10 hp Rolls-Royce cars had the classic Rolls-Royce radiator, though the 'entwined-Rs' badge did not appear until a little later. This is the first such car (ie the third Rolls-Royce car), chassis 20152. The rear-entrance tonneau coachwork was built by Barker & Co, the coachbuilder favoured by C. S. Rolls & Co.

1905 Rolls-Royce 10 hp, chassis 20162. The oval badge on the radiators of some of these very early cars (some had no badge at all) bore the words 'The Rolls-Royce Radiator'. 20162 survives and may be seen in the Science Museum, South Kensington, London.

This later example of the 10 hp, chassis 20165, used a longer-wheelbase (8 ft 1 in) chassis with integral front dumb-irons in place of the less satisfactory bolted-on variety seen on the Royce and earlier Rolls-Royce 10 hp chassis. The final two 10 hp cars had a 7 ft 4½ in wheelbase chassis believed to have been left surplus following the cancellation of the Bonnetless Town Carriage project. Though long reputed to be a 1905 model, 20165 was in fact delivered in early 1907. It is owned by the Company, to whom it was presented in 1920 by Mr S. J. Gammell, who drove it from Aberdeen to Derby for the presentation.

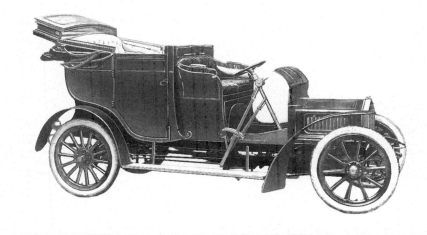

The 'odd man out' in the original Rolls-Royce range of cars was the 15 hp, which used three separate cylinder castings rather than pairs as on the other models. This is chassis 24273, a 1905 15 hp with Barker landaulette coachwork, exhibited before its engine was fitted at the Paris Salon at the end of 1904, then at the London Motor Show at Olympia in February 1905.

1906 chassis 26332, seen at the Derby factory towards the end of its working life. This car was delivered new to Paris Singer (son of Isaac Singer of sewing-machine fame) who had also been the first customer to take delivery of a Rolls-Royce (though the second chassis number), 10 hp 20151.

The stand of C. S. Rolls & Co at the 1905 Olympia Motor Show, held in February of that year. At the left is a 30 hp six-cylinder Rolls-Royce, chassis 24274, while to the right is 15 hp three-cylinder 24273. Note that the address of C. S. Rolls & Co at that time was what is still the London showroom of Rolls-Royce Motor Cars Ltd today.

The Rolls-Royce showroom at 14-15 Conduit Street, seen in 1956. Silver Cloud and Bentley S Type cars are on display.

This photograph of the very early Rolls-Royce steering wheel shows that right from the outset Royce eschewed the use of the words 'advance' and `retard' for the ignition timing control, believing that chauffeurs would be confused; he preferred 'early' and 'late'. The quadrant plate on which the controls were mounted turned with the steering wheel on the earliest cars.

Royce already had other more ambitious models on the drawing-board, and the agreement with Rolls specified a range of models to be produced. By grouping three separate 4-inch by 5-inch cylinders, a 3,000 cc 15 hp car was evolved, to satisfy Rolls's requirement for a three-cylinder model. Royce more logically developed two further models, a four-cylinder 20 hp and a six-cylinder 30 hp, by grouping pairs of cylinders similar to those used for the 10 hp, and in so doing was able to standardise many of the moving parts.

A fifth, even more interesting engine was designed and built for use in the 'bonnetless' (or 'Invisible') town carriages and the 'Legalimit', both of which Royce had been prevailed upon to build in response to perceived demand. This was a 3,500 cc V-8, one of the first V-8 engines and obviously wasted on the ponderous machines for which it was designed. The eight cylinders were arranged in a 90-degree vee formation, and although it could have been designed to take the same standard cylinder blocks as the two-, four- and six-cylinder cars, entirely different blocks were used with vertical valves; that is to say, the valves were arranged at 45 degrees to the cylinders. The bore and stroke were the same at 3¼ inches. Only two of the 'Invisible Engine' or 'bonnetless' town carriages were completed and, mercifully, only one 'Legalimit', which was deliberately designed to be so low-geared as to be incapable of exceeding the then ruling speed limit of 20 mph. The one-model policy of 1908 unfortunately spelled the end for Royce's V-8, otherwise it would have been interesting to have seen what could have been made of such an advanced engine.

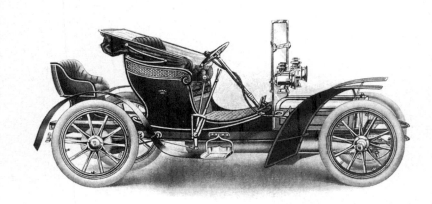

As its name suggests, the 'Legalimit' was designed to run at a speed not exceeding the then prevailing UK speed limit, which had recently been raised to a dizzy 20 mph. The car was powered by Royce's most remarkable engine of the period, a V-8 of 3,500 cc capacity – which must inescapably be seen as a rather absurd under-utilisation of an advanced and potentially powerful engine for its period. Only one Legalimit was completed, chassis 40518, and was delivered to Baron Northcliffe in 1906, who returned it within six months as part payment on a 40/50. The same engine was used, rather more logically, to power the 'bonnetless' (or 'Invisible') town carriage of the same period (1905-06), its comparatively flat shape facilitating its fitting under the floor. Both models were cancelled after only a handful of cars had been completed, and the V-8 engine never saw its full potential.

Rolls showed a preference for the four-cylinder model and, backed by his sporting enthusiasm, Rolls-Royce cars quickly made a name for themselves in motor racing, with Percy Northey's 'Light' 20 hp Rolls-Royce taking second place in the 1905 Isle of Man Tourist Trophy. Two Light Twenties were entered, but the second, in the hands of C. S. Rolls, suffered a smashed gearbox less than a mile from the start, almost certainly due to his attempt to engage a gear after coasting – though at the time sabotage was strongly hinted at!

However, in the following year's TT Rolls was able to redeem himself and further enhance the name of Rolls-Royce by bringing his car over the finishing line in first place, at an average speed of 39.3 mph.

With such a range of designs at their disposal it might seem odd that Rolls-Royce soon saw fit to abandon all of them, from the little 10 hp up to the powerful 30 hp six, until one considers the very magnificence of the 40/50 hp model on which the Company's 'one-model' policy of 1908 was based.

Right from the outset Royce Ltd, then Rolls-Royce Ltd, established a set of principles that have guided the succeeding makers of The Best Car in the World to this day. These principles are difficult to define in the written word and are based firmly upon Royce's own impatience with mediocrity. Yet once he had something that worked well he was reluctant to change for change's sake; any new design had to be shown conclusively to be superior to the old. This conservatism has come to personify Rolls-Royce, yet the Company has not

The most successful of the early Rolls-Royce cars was the four-cylinder 20 hp, which was made in 'Light' and 'Heavy' guises. C. S. Rolls raced this model with conspicuous success in the Isle of Man Tourist Trophy and elsewhere and is seen here driving a Light Twenty, chassis 26350B, in the 1906 Isle of Man TT, in which he came first at an average speed of 39.3 mph.

shrunk from embodying bold and innovative ideas into its cars once they have been proven.

Despite this reputation for cautious conservatism, Rolls-Royce was always innovative. Look, for example, at the throttle governor fitted to the 40/50 hp Rolls-Royce cars. Although the control on the steering wheel boss looked like an ordinary hand throttle, as on lesser cars, this ingenious device was actually more akin to today's 'cruise control' in that it could be used to maintain automatically any given road speed up hill and down. It was also a boon to quiet gear changing, once the principle was mastered. It only disappeared from the 40/50 hp models when synchromesh was adopted in the early 1930s.

The torsional vibration damper, or 'slipper drive', was an invention of Royce aimed at alleviating the vibration periods to which his 30 hp engine, like all in-line six-cylinder engines, was prone. As an example of great minds thinking alike, Dr Frederick Lanchester discovered the same idea at around the same time. Lanchester was astute enough to patent the idea, but Royce was able to demonstrate that he had used the damper on a car before Lanchester and an agreement was struck between the two companies, by which Rolls-Royce would not contest the patent if Lanchester did not pursue royalties from Rolls-Royce.

The Rolls-Royce radiator shape, which remained basically unchanged from the earliest models to those made at Crewe today, is probably the most obvious example of Rolls-Royce being steeped in tradition.

Four-cylinder 20 hp Rolls-Royce cars under construction in the chassis erecting bay at the Cooke Street, Manchester, works of Royce Ltd, where the three Royce cars and the earliest Rolls-Royce cars were built. Note the Royce electric bell over the doorway at the top of the stairs on the right, which led to Royce's office.

In an uncharacteristic misjudgment, Henry Royce wanted to abandon the traditional radiator design as long ago as the late 1920s, but the astute General Manager Claude Johnson successfully argued for its retention. The modern Rolls-Royce 'radiator' is a dummy shell hand-soldered from stainless steel sheet.

Royce himself is on record as wanting to abandon it on the grounds that the famous sharp-edged structure was impractical, unnecessarily costly to make and of no value aerodynamically. In this he was absolutely right, as he usually was, and specialised craftsmen have to be employed to this day to hand-solder stainless steel sheets to form what has long since become the dummy header tank and radiator sides. Yet how right of the General Manager, the shrewd Claude Johnson, to use his influence to retain it, reasoning that it had become too distinctive a feature of Rolls-Royce cars to be recklessly abandoned.

Rolls-Royce has never balked at using other manufacturers' ideas where these offer a satisfactory solution to its needs. An obvious example of this is the classic Rolls-Royce friction-disc brake servo. This was adopted in 1925 and remained (on the Phantom VI) right up to the end of the 1970s. This ingenious system comprised a clutch-like device driven by the gearbox and coupled to the brake rigging through a system of rods, with hydraulic circuits progressively incorporated after the Second World War, to harness the car's own momentum to assist the rear braking and apply the front brakes. This system was developed after extensive testing of an Hispano Suiza equipped with a transmission-driven drum-type servo. It overcame Royce's objection to front-wheel brakes – the inability of locked front wheels to steer the car – by so balancing the front and rear braking efforts that the rear wheels would always lock first, stopping the transmission (and therefore the servo) and releasing the front brakes. Effectively, this was an early form of anti-lock brakes!

Rolls-Royce owes the design of its independent front suspension, first seen late in 1935 on the Phantom III, to the General Motors Corporation. The choice followed years of investigation into various i.f.s. systems then available, of which the GM 'knee-action' design proved most suitable. After the Second World War a simpler system of independent front suspension was borrowed from the contemporary Packard, but built much more substantially and with greater refinement by Rolls-Royce. Later, the GM automatic transmission was adopted, at first fully bought out, then built at Crewe and finally again fully bought out.

Royce preferred to build practically every part of the car rather than buying proprietary components. Even the electrics, including the starter and dynamo, and other engine ancillaries were manufactured in-house. An end to this practice began with the Springfield-built Silver Ghosts, for which American-made (Bosch, Westinghouse, etc) electrical components were progressively adopted. After Royce's death in 1933 the Rolls-Royce board at home began to see the wisdom of this. The late 20/25s had a Borg & Beck clutch, the Phantom III and 25/30 had Stromberg carburetters, and after the war all models used Lucas Special Equipment starters, dynamos and other electrical components. Nowadays the starter motor and air conditioning compressor are of Japanese manufacture – a sign of the times.

Royce's influence on the design of the cars remained profound right up until, and arguably after, his death. His failing health had obliged him to work from his summer home at West Wittering in Sussex and his winter home at Le Canadel, in the south of France, yet he remained Chief Engineer until he died.

As a personal partnership, the link between Rolls and Royce lasted only six years, having been cut short by the untimely death of the 33-year-old Rolls in a flying accident in 1910. The linking of the names, however, remained unaffected by the tragic accident, and had fate not dealt such a cruel blow Rolls would no doubt have been totally delighted with the later involvement of Rolls-Royce in aero engine production, particularly as the Company that bore his name excelled in that field so conspicuously.

PRE-SILVER GHOST MODELS, 1904–1907

Model	Year	Bore	Stroke	c.c.	h.p.	Clutch	Gearbox	Final Drive	Suspension	Brakes	Wheelbase	Track	Number Made	Chassis Made
2-cylinder	1904-1905 1906	3¾" 3¹⁵⁄₁₆"	5" 5"	1,800 2,000	10	Leather-lined cone type.	Three-speed	Fully-floating live axle. Spur-type gears.	Semi-elliptic	Transmission foot-brake. Handbrake operates on rear wheels.	6' 3" (early) 8' 1" (late)	4' 0"	3 Royce 16 Rolls-Royce.	£395
3-cylinder	1905	4"	5"	3,000	15	Leather-lined cone type.	Three-speed	Fully-floating live axle. Spur-type gears.	Semi-elliptic.	Transmission foot-brake. Handbrake operates on rear wheels.	8' 7"		6	£500
4-cylinder	1905 1905-1906	3¾" 4"	5" 5"	3,600 4,000	20	Leather-lined cone type.	Heavy model three-speed. Light model four-speed (overdrive fourth).		Semi-elliptic front. Platform rear.	Transmission foot-brake. Handbrake operates on rear wheels.	Light model 8' 10" Heavy model 9' 6"	Light model 4' 8" Heavy model 4' 8"	40	£650
6-cylinder	1905-1906		5"	6,000	30	Leather-lined cone type.	Four-speed (overdrive fourth).		Semi-elliptic front. Platform rear.	Transmission foot-brake. Handbrake operates on rear wheels.	Short Wheelbase 9' 8½" Long Wheelbase 9' 10"	4' 8"	37	£890
'Legalimit' and Bonnetless V-8's	1905-1906	3¾"	3¾"	3,500		Leather-lined cone type.	Three-speed.		Semi-elliptic.	Transmission foot-brake. Handbrake operates on rear wheels.	Bonnetless 7' 6" 'Legalimit' 8' 10"	4' 4"	2 Bonnetless cars 1 Legalimit	

Chapter Two

The Silver Ghost
and the One-Model Policy

The manufacturing and marketing agreement between Royce Ltd and C. S. Rolls & Co remained in force for a little over a year, after which a new company, Rolls-Royce Ltd, was registered, with £60,000 capital, on 16 March 1906. The directors of the new company were Rolls, Royce, A. H. Briggs and Claude Johnson from C. S. Rolls & Co, with Claremont as Chairman and John de Looze from Royce Ltd as Secretary. C. S. Rolls & Co. was dissolved and the Conduit Street, London W1, offices and showroom and the workshop at Lillie Hall, Fulham, were transferred to the new Company. At first Rolls-Royce Ltd had no manufacturing facilities and for the time being the cars were still built at the Manchester works of Royce Ltd, which remained independent and was not absorbed by the new Company.

Late in 1906 the 40/50 hp Rolls-Royce was introduced to the world at the Olympia Motor Show in London; the first chassis to be seen by the public was displayed alongside a 30 hp Barker limousine on the stand of C. S. Rolls & Co. The new model was destined to make a more profound impression on the motoring world than any other motor car in history that comes readily to mind. The 40/50 differed from its six-cylinder predecessor, the 30 hp, chiefly in its larger size and in its engine, which was a side valve unit of 4½-inch bore and stroke, with its cylinders cast in two blocks of three rather than three pairs.

The following year the 12th 40/50 chassis to be completed (60551) was selected by Claude Johnson and fitted with a handsome touring body by Barker & Co. With its aluminium paint and silver-plated lamps and fittings, this car earned the name 'The Silver Ghost', a name that it still carries on an engraved plate attached to the front of the dash. Thus a complete 40/50 car was exhibited at the 1907 Motor Show.

The Rolls-Royce 40/50 h.p. quickly established itself as the ultimate in luxury motoring, and a press report of the period called it 'The Best Car in the World' – a richly deserved compliment with firm foundation in fact and one that has stuck ever since.

'The Silver Ghost' became a C. S. Rolls & Co demonstration vehicle, and its reliability and stamina were put to the test in a 2,000-mile trial under the supervision of the Royal Automobile Club. During this trial a petrol economy figure of better than 20 miles per gallon was achieved on the road between London and Glasgow – quite a feat for a large car with an engine capacity in excess of 7 litres. Following this effort 'The Silver Ghost' was entered in the Scottish Reliability Trial. After 629 miles the only involuntary stop was almost certainly caused by a failure to re-open the petrol tap after an overnight stop. However, to save face a legend was cultivated that the tap shook itself shut on the rough roads, in fact a virtual impossibility. Either way, after the brief halt 'The Silver Ghost' continued to run, resting only on Sundays, until 15,000 miles had been covered; 14,371 miles had therefore been driven without an involuntary stop – a world record. The cost of the parts required to return the car to as-new condition was £2 2s 7d.

On 9 July 1908 a fine new

There is no doubt that Royce's masterpiece was the 40/50 hp model, the first examples of which were turned out from Cooke Street in time for a chassis to be exhibited at the 1906 Olympia Motor Show. For the following year's show the 12th 40/50 chassis, 60551, was fitted by Barker & Co with magnificent tourer coachwork, painted in aluminium paint with all fittings silver-plated. This car wore (and still wears) a name-plate bearing the name 'The Silver Ghost', which much later became the type name for the 40/50 hp model. 60551 distinguished itself as a Company demonstration car and was re-acquired by the Company in 1948 when it was fortuitously taken as part exchange on a new Bentley Mk VI. It is still owned by Rolls-Royce Motor Cars Ltd today and remains a powerful publicity tool.

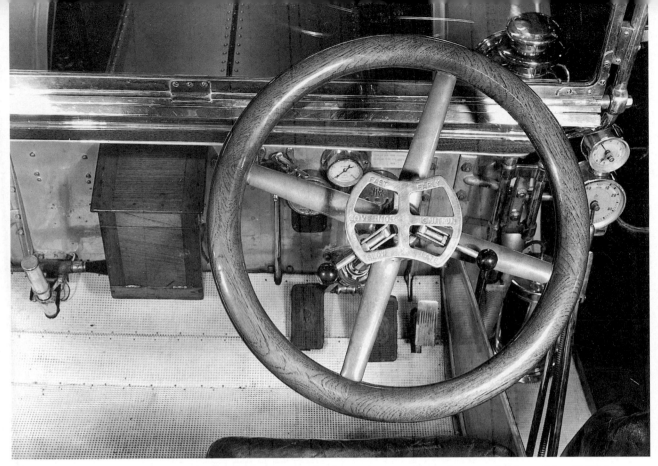

Chassis 60551. In comparison with the early steering wheel seen in a previous photograph, that of the 40/50 hp was a much more elegant and sophisticated affair. Unlike that of the earlier models, the quadrant for the controls in the centre of the wheel was arranged so that it remained stationary when the wheel was turned. Also, the hand throttle had become a superbly made governor, which in addition to being an effective aid to silent gear changing was capable of maintaining a given road speed up hill and down dale, much the same in effect as the 'cruise control' of today's cars.

This cut-away drawing of 60551 shows the chassis features of the early 40/50 hp Rolls-Royce. The rear suspension of the earliest 40/50s was by 'platform' springing – ie semi-elliptic leaf springs shackled to the chassis at their leading edges and linked at the rear by an inverted transverse leaf spring. This arrangement quickly gave way to three-quarter elliptic springs, which in effect meant that the transverse spring was cut in half, turned forward through 90 degrees and anchored to the rear of the frame side members. Many more changes to the initial design were introduced over the 20-year production run.

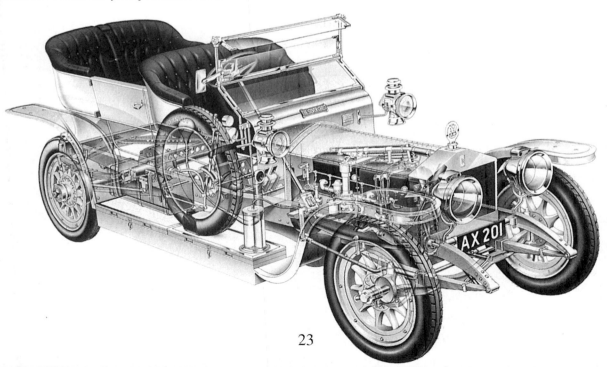

Early 40/50 hp cars at the Cat & Fiddle inn, near Buxton, Derbyshire, on 22 June 1907. From left to right they are: chassis 60551 ('The Silver Ghost') with Claude Johnson, Managing Director, Rolls-Royce Ltd, at the wheel; chassis 60539, Charles Rolls at the wheel; chassis 60540, Harry J. Swindley of The Autocar at the wheel; and chassis 60566, test driver W. Hallam at the wheel. The cars were en route to Scotland for the Scottish Reliability Trial.

In 1957 Rolls-Royce Ltd joined a group of enthusiasts to re-enact the Cat & Fiddle meeting. From left to right in this view the cars are: chassis 60551 ('The Silver Ghost'); chassis 60588, owned by Adrian Garrett and now in New Zealand, still in his ownership; chassis 60577 ('The Auld Lady'), owned by J. P. Smith; and chassis 1278, owned by Jack Barclay Ltd.

'Spirit of Ecstasy has selected road travel as her supreme delight and has alighted on the prow of a Rolls-Royce car to revel in the freshness of the air and the musical sound of her fluttering draperies' – Charles Sykes. The company was becoming increasingly concerned at the tasteless mascots appearing on all too many British cars, including those of their manufacture, so celebrated artist Charles Sykes was commissioned to design a suitable standard mascot for the Rolls-Royce car. The result was the Spirit of Ecstasy and in 1911 it was announced that 'arrangements are being made whereby an owner of a Rolls-Royce may acquire one of these figureheads for a few pounds'. Under this agreement the copyright of the Spirit of Ecstasy was owned by Rolls-Royce Ltd and Sykes was to be the sole maker of the mascot for as long as he was able. It subsequently became as much an instantly recognised feature of the Rolls-Royce car as the famous radiator and the entwined R's monogram.

The first car to be fitted with the Spirit of Ecstasy radiator mascot was this 1910 Silver Ghost, chassis 1404, delivered with Barker tourer coachwork to Lord Montagu of Beaulieu, who was a director of Rolls-Royce Ltd. Conventional wisdom has it that Eleanor Thornton, Lord Montagu's secretary, was the model for the mascot, and there is strong circumstantial evidence that Sykes's experience of the silent performance of the 1404 provided the inspiration. In any case it is certain that the histories of 1404 and the Spirit of Ecstasy are inextricably intermixed. After a sojourn in India with Lord Montagu, 1404 eventually found its way to Australia where it is undergoing a comprehensive restoration in the hands of owner Ian Irwin. Note the large (and very expensive) Palmer Cord tyres.

The 40/50 hp chassis proved completely suitable for all forms of coachwork from the most sporting to the most formal. This 1912 Silver Ghost, chassis 1850E, has spacious limousine coachwork by Thrupp & Maberly.

A 1912 Silver Ghost, chassis 1853E, restored by South Australian enthusiast Eric Rainsford. By this time electric lighting had become the norm. Wire wheels were often specified instead of wooden.

Rolls-Royce motor car factory was opened in Derby by Lord Montagu of Beaulieu. Although a quite comprehensive range of chassis had been built at Manchester, with two, three, four and six cylinders – and even a V-8 – production at Derby was to be concentrated on the magnificent 40/50 hp six-cylinder car, which was subsequently to become known as the Silver Ghost type, all other models being discontinued. This one-model policy was instigated by Managing Director Claude Johnson, who saw no

point in continuing to offer a proliferation of models when one superlative model stood out from the remainder of the range.

The Silver Ghost was built from late 1906, when the first few chassis were built at Manchester, through to 1926, when the last chassis were built by the Company's American subsidiary in Springfield, Massachusetts. During this remarkable 20-year production run, some 7,876 Silver Ghost chassis were built at Manchester (the very

early cars), Derby (the vast majority) and Springfield (the Springfield cars, mainly for North American consumption).

Various modified versions of the Silver Ghost were tried. The first of these was never offered to the public because Royce considered the four modified cars too coarse and noisy, though Charles Rolls used one and is said to have thought very highly of it. The power output of these four cars, rated at 70 hp, was increased by raising the compression ratio and

1912 Silver Ghost chassis 1907 with Barker Pullman limousine coachworks. This car, now in the USA, was the subject of a well-known Corgi model which, like the original, is a sought-after collector's item.

27

A 1912 London-to-Edinburgh type Silver Ghost, chassis 1884. HRH The Prince of Wales (later King Edward VIII) is seen in the rear seat and the Royal Standard is flying on the radiator cap. The tourer coachwork was built by Mulliners of Birmingham, and the photograph was taken at Duntroon House in Canberra during the 1920 Royal Tour of Australia. The London-to-Edinburgh type Silver Ghost was characterised by cantilever rear springs in lieu of the standard three-quarter elliptics. On the earliest examples these were fitted under the axle – ie 'underslung'.

Beginning (experimentally) with London Trials car chassis 1948, seen here at the Derby works, the cantilever rear springs of the London-to-Edinburgh type cars were fitted over the axle instead of under it. What we know today as the London-to-Edinburgh type chassis was not described as such on chassis cards and build records but rather as a 'duplicate of 1701' – the original London-to-Edinburgh car. The sporting tourer coachwork of this example, by Holmes of Derby, may be regarded as typical of the type, though some L-E type chassis were fitted with coachwork of a more formal nature.

This 1913 London-to-Edinburgh type car, chassis 2260, was entered by the Company in the 1913 Austrian Alpine Trial, in which the Rolls-Royce cars triumphed so splendidly. The extension tube under the radiator cap helped to avoid water loss due to expansion on the long Alpine ascents. The Austrian Alpine cars were also fitted with four-speed gearboxes with an extra-low first gear to avoid a repetition of James Radley's balking episode the previous year. Production chassis of this specification were known as the 'Alpine Eagle' type.

1922 Silver Ghost chassis 33KG, an H. J. Mulliner tourer, photographed in 1945 when used by HRH The Duke of Gloucester, then Governor-General of Australia. Note the vice-regal crown on the front of the car

"THE Car was taken from rest to nearly seventy miles an hour on its top gear, and for every purpose of our journey might well have had no other. . . . Our travel was one of smooth acceleration and deceleration . . . with silence under the bonnet and a calm inside the car that spoke eloquently of perfect condition and balance in the engine and a suspension which neither speed nor pot-hole could jar."

The Field, February 18th, 1922.

ROLLS-ROYCE, LIMITED,
15, CONDUIT STREET, LONDON, W.I.

Telegrams: *Telephone:*
Roihead, Picey., *Mayfair 6040*
London. *'4 lines'.*

other mechanical changes including overhead inlet valves. Two of the experimental 70 hp cars, named Silver Rogue and White Knave, were entered in the 1908 International and Scottish six-day Touring Car Trial, a 2,000-mile event in which Silver Rogue won its Class.

In 1909 the stroke of the 40/50 hp engine was increased to 4¾ inches, raising the cubic capacity from 7,036 cc to 7,428 cc. In the same year the four-speed overdrive gearbox was changed to a three-speed box with the direct drive on third gear in order, it is said, to overcome the propensity of owners to drive continuously in the (overdrive) fourth gear.

The next modified version of the Silver Ghost was the London-to-Edinburgh model, introduced in 1911. This model derived from chassis 1701, which was fitted with underslung cantilever rear springs, a raised compression ratio and a larger carburetter for an RAC-observed, top-gear-only, non-stop trial run between London and Edinburgh, a distance of some 400 miles. The purpose of this trial was to put paid to the extravagant claims of the then rival Napier company, one of whose 65 hp cars had recently completed a similar test over the same route. The

Rolls-Royce proved superior in both top speed and fuel economy, returning a remarkable 24.32 miles per gallon, and later, without alteration or adjustment, a speed of 78.26 mph on the Brooklands track. Later in 1911 the same chassis fitted with a streamlined racing body attained a speed of 101.8 mph at Brooklands. The car could also nevertheless be driven at a walking pace in top gear! Many Silver Ghosts with the London-to-Edinburgh specification were fitted with narrow, low-waisted, sporting bodies of often singularly handsome lines. Nowadays, genuine London-to-Edinburgh Silver Ghosts are among the most highly prized of all Rolls-Royce cars.

In the 1912 Austrian Alpine Trials, in an embarrassing episode for the Company, chassis 1930E, a London-to-Edinburgh type 40/50 hp driven by James Radley, balked on one of the steeper passes. Though in retrospect this was caused by Radley's choice of an 18/52 final drive which over-geared the car for the 1 in 4 passes of the Alpine Trial, Royce immediately set about designing a four-speed gearbox with an extra-low-ratio first gear to avoid a repetition. The following year three Silver Ghost entries, all with the new four-speed

gearboxes, taller radiators and increased ground clearance, comprehensively vanquished all opposition in a glorious high point in Rolls-Royce history. This success has been commemorated twice – first in 1973, and again in 1993 – by gruelling re-enactments that demonstrated the longevity, strength and stamina of the marque and particularly of the Silver Ghost model. The special Alpine version of the Silver Ghost that achieved the 1913 success was at first called the 'Continental' model, but the name that captured the imagination and has stuck is 'Alpine Eagle'.

During the First World War Silver Ghosts performed valiantly in a variety of wartime roles, including ambulances, staff cars and, as any reader of T. E. Lawrence's Seven Pillars of Wisdom will know, as military tenders and armoured cars. The remarkable armoured cars covered many thousands of trouble-free miles in the most appalling desert conditions, their inefficiently filtered carburetters breathing desert sand and their radiators coping with extremes of heat and cold while burdened with many times the weight for which the chassis was designed.

After the war the Silver Ghost was put back into production. Almost the entire electrical system, including the then new electric starter, was designed and manufactured by Rolls-Royce. Various other improvements were introduced, including, at the end of 1923, four-wheel brakes with the now famous mechanical friction disc servo.

In 1925, with the New Phantom in production, Derby ceased production of the Silver Ghost. However, Silver Ghost production continued for another year or so at Springfield, Massachusetts, where Claude Johnson had opened a new factory in 1919 to build Rolls-Royce chassis for the increasingly important North American market. During the remarkable production run of nearly 20 years the chassis price almost doubled, from £980 in 1907 to £1,850 in 1923.

TECHNICAL SPECIFICATION

40/50 hp Silver Ghost, 1906-1925

Engine

Six cylinders in line, cast in two blocks of three. Aluminium crankcase.
Bore 4½ inches, stroke 4½ inches, cubic capacity 7,036 cc. Side valves with single camshaft. Seven-bearing crankshaft. Royce two-jet carburetter.

1909: Stroke 4¾ inches, cubic capacity 7,428 cc.

Chassis

Channel-section side-members with tubular cross-members.
Overall length 15 ft 0 in short chassis, 15 ft 7¼ in long chassis. Wheelbase 11 ft 3½ in short chassis, 11 ft 11½ in long chassis.
1914: Overall length 15 ft 10¼ in. Wheelbase, 11 ft 11½ in.
1923: Overall length 15 ft 10¼ in short chassis, 16 ft 4¾ in long chassis. Wheelbase 12 ft 0 in short chassis, 12 ft 6½ in long chassis.

Transmission

Leather-lined cone-type clutch. Four-speed gearbox with overdrive fourth gear. Right-hand control.
Open propeller shaft, radius rods to control rear axle.

1909: Three-speed gearbox.
1911: Propeller shaft enclosed in torque tube.
1913: Four-speed gearbox, direct-drive fourth gear.

Steering

Worm and nut.

Suspension

Semi-elliptic front, platform rear.

1908: Three-quarter-elliptic rear springs.
1911: London-to-Edinburgh type cars, cantilever rear springs.
1912: Cantilever rear springs standard.

Brakes

External contracting brake on transmission operated by foot pedal; handbrake operating on rear drums.

1913: Footbrake concentric with handbrake on rear drums.
1924: Four-wheel brakes operated by friction disc servo driven by gearbox.

Fuel system

Petrol tank under front seat, gravity feed assisted by exhaust pressure.
1909: Tank mounted in rear of chassis, pressurised by gearbox-driven air pump and hand pump for starting.
1919: Air pump on distributor drive.
1924: Autovac.

Road wheels and tyres

Wooden-spoked wheels standard, 10 spokes front, 14 rear.
1909: Wire wheels optional. Wooden wheels continued to be available until 1921.

Springfield Silver Ghost, 1921-1926, was similar at first but changes were introduced as follows:

1925: Left-hand drive, three-speed gearbox, centre change.

CHASSIS NUMBERS

Chassis numbers	Year
60539-60542	1906-07
60544-60592	1907
60700-60799	1907-08
919-1015	1908-09
1100-2699	1909-13

In 1913 alphanumeric chassis numbers were introduced, with a number followed by a letter suffix as follows. The number 13 was not used.

	Year
CA	1913
NA	1913-14
MA, AB, EB, RB, PB, YB, UB, LB, GB	1914
TB	1914-15
BD, AD, ED	1915
RD	1915-16
CB, PD, AC	1916
PP, LW	1919
TW, CW, FW, BW, AE, EE, RE, PE, YE	1920
WO	1920-27 (Armoured car chassis)
UE, LE	1921
GE	1920-21
TE, CE, NE	1921
AG, LG, MG, JG, UG, SG	1921-22
TG, KG, PG, RG, YG	1922
ZG, HG	1922-23
LK, NK, PK	1923
EM	1923-24
LM, RM, TM	1924
AU, EU	1924-25

Springfield used certain numbers in the CE to KG series inclusive, then used XH, HH and JH. They then duplicated some of the LK and PK series, adding an 'S' prefix, and added MK, RK, FK, ML, PL, RL, all with the 'S' prefix.

Total: 6,173 Manchester and Derby cars, 1,703 Springfield cars.

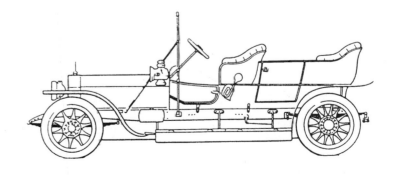

31

Chapter Three

The Twenty, its successors, and the Bentleys

As well as serving their country in war, 40/50 hp Silver Ghosts served the Company very well and seem to have more than satisfied their customers, remaining the only model (with variants such as the London-to-Edinburgh type) until 1922 when the 'small' Rolls-Royce, the Twenty Horsepower, was introduced. With its overhead valve six-cylinder engine and other modern features, the Twenty accentuated the Silver Ghost's Edwardian origins.

The chassis frame of the Twenty, with channel-section side rails and tubular cross-members, was fairly unremarkable in appearance, although its structural integrity was proven by means of the Experimental Department's 'bumping machine' – a punishing device that was said to crowd 'ten years into a single day'.

The engine, of a little over 3 litres capacity, was a pushrod overhead valve unit with cast iron cylinder head and block and aluminium alloy crankcase. A departure from the Silver Ghost, which represented modern practice and was perfectly logical, but which lacked the enthusiastic support of both customers and the motoring press, was the three-speed gearbox with centre-change lever. So poor a reception did this modern feature receive that later, when four-wheel brakes were introduced and a new gearbox had to be designed in any case to take the brake servo, the opportunity was taken to change to a four-speed box with right-hand gate change. Whilst it must be admitted

The chassis of the Twenty Horsepower as introduced in 1922, reproduced from The Autocar of 13 October of that year. The nearside chassis rail and the centre cross-members have been 'cut away' to reveal other details of the chassis. Note the three-speed gearbox in unit with the engine and the centre ball-type gear-change and handbrake lever.

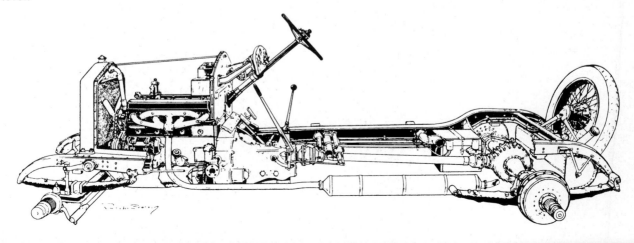

A standard range of bodies was designed by Ivan Evernden for the Twenty. These bodies were built by outside coachbuilders, notably Barker and, increasingly, Park Ward. This is the tourer as offered in the sales catalogue of the time.

that this new gear change, with its almost miniature gate, unlike the large, notched gate of the Silver Ghost, was an absolute delight, it is arguable whether the Twenty actually needed four forward speeds. However, a four-speed gearbox was expected on an expensive car, whether it needed it or not!

Another fairly controversial feature of the Twenty was the use of the 'Hotchkiss drive', with open propeller shaft and the rear axle located by the semi-elliptic springs. Together with the three-speed gearbox with ball-type centre change, this was seen as an American feature, and a cheap and nasty one at that. Royce, however, was perfectly satisfied with it, and with the Twenty Horsepower design as a whole. In

Later Twenties had four-wheel servo brakes and a four-speed gearbox with side levers. This is chassis GMJ52, a 1926 tourer by H. J. Mulliner delivered new to Miss L. Overend of Dublin and driven by her as regular transport until well into the 1980s.

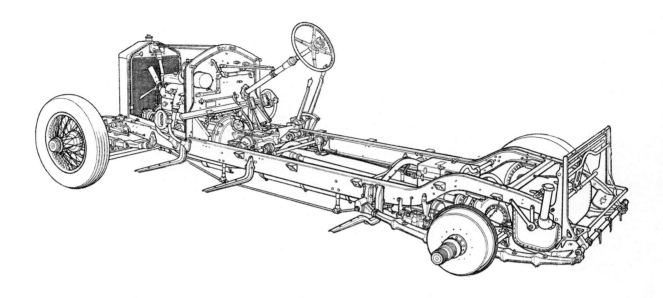

The chassis of the earliest 20/25s, introduced in 1929, differed from the last 20 hp cars only in respect to the engine. This is the 20/25 chassis as shown in the 15 October 1929 edition of The Motor.

fact, he once asked his friend and biographer Sir Max Pemberton, 'Can you tell me a better car?'

The Twenty, of course, had the same radiator shape as the Silver Ghost. Early Twenties, however, had radiused edges to the radiator header tank, which gave it a subtly different appearance from the sharp-edged structure of that of the Silver Ghost. The Twenty also differed in having a set of horizontal radiator shutters operated by a hand lever on the instrument board to assist warm-up in cold conditions (though the Springfield Silver Ghost had acquired similar shutters soon after its introduction). On the Twenty these were at first enamelled in black, but were later changed to German silver to match the radiator shell.

Whilst the Twenty was well received by the motoring press of the time, it must be said that features such as the centre-change gearbox were described with less than enthusiasm. *The Autocar*, for example, was polite

The small-horsepower chassis was particularly well suited to owner-driver coachwork. This early 20/25 has foursome drophead coupé coachwork by Park Ward.

The Bentley 3½ Litre was the first Bentley designed and built by Rolls-Royce. Nearly all Derby Bentley chassis were fitted with owner-driver saloon bodies or sporting drophead coupes. In these two views the saloon (left) *and the drophead coupe represent the standard designs offered by Park Ward.*

about it, but became conspicuously more enthusiastic when the later version was introduced. To quote its 22 January 1926 road test: 'The latest model of the 20 hp Rolls-Royce is a very considerable improvement on its predecessors. A four-speed gear box, right-hand gear lever, servo-operated four wheel brakes, and a number of small details have made the car altogether different from the first model, and it is now much more a smaller edition of the larger car which has made the car world-famous'. The new gear change was singled out for particular praise, which was well deserved as the change is utterly delightful. The Company obviously listened, because once having reverted to the right-hand gate gear change it remained a feature of all Rolls-Royce cars, save for left-hand-drive chassis and a few Bentley Continentals, right through to the post-Second World War period and the advent of automatic transmission, after other manufacturers had long since abandoned it in favour of the cheaper centre change and the woeful steering column change.

The Twenty was and still is a car of considerable charm. Its performance, which was perfectly adequate in its time, is somewhat lacking in a modern context, but this is more than compensated for in smoothness, silence, refinement and sheer driving pleasure. It formed the basis of a line of progressively more powerful and

even more refined Rolls-Royce cars, culminating in the Wraith of 1938, and of the contemporary Bentley models.

Alongside the three pre-war Phantoms and the Bentley models the small-horsepower Rolls-Royce grew in engine capacity from the 3,127 cc of the Twenty Horsepower to 3,699 cc, to become the 20/25 hp (1929), then to 4,257 cc to become the 25/30 hp (1936).

The earliest 20/25s were identical in chassis details to the final production of the Twenty, the larger-capacity engine with new cross-flow cylinder head being the only distinguishing feature, and the two models were produced side by side during 1929. The Twenty had by then received vertical radiator shutters like those of the Phantoms, and the 20/25 followed suit.

The 20/25 model was developed alongside its larger stablemate, the Phantom II, acquiring many of the features developed for that model, such as thermostatically operated radiator shutters, one-shot chassis lubrication and synchromesh on third and top gears (1932) and a new single-jet expanding-type carburetter (1934).

By the end of the 1920s the Rolls-Royce motor car was firmly established as *The Best Car in the World*. There were, however, many other fine marques of undoubted merit. Among these was the Bentley, a marque usually associated with the

big green tourers that were raced with such spectacular success at Le Mans and elsewhere, but which was also penetrating the formal limousine market sufficiently successfully to give rise to some disquiet at Derby.

However, the rapidly deteriorating economic climate of the period, which Rolls-Royce Ltd was able to weather, brought about a rapid reversal in the fortunes of Bentley Motors Ltd, and by 1931, with their financial backers becoming nervous and the Depression biting deeply, the firm was in the hands of a receiver. On 10 September of that year Bentley Motors Ltd was voluntarily liquidated.

Another great British marque, the Napier, had passed into history, its makers having turned their attention to aero engines instead. In 1931, however, D. Napier & Son, having decided to return to motor car manufacturing, began negotiations with Bentley Motors for the purchase of that company with the view to building a Napier-Bentley car, with W. O. Bentley in charge of design. W. O. Bentley was naturally enthusiastic about this proposal, as it would mean the salvation of the Bentley car embodying his unique design philosophy, if not of Bentley Motors Ltd itself.

The take-over of Bentley Motors by Napier seemed a *fait accompli* but for the formalities. Then, at the eleventh hour, fate took a different

A 1935 Bentley 3½ Litre saloon by Thrupp & Maberly, chassis B64DG.

The 20/25 chassis was perhaps best suited to closer-coupled saloon coachwork, of which this Park Ward 'Continental Sports Saloon' is a particularly attractive example. Chassis GRC56 owned by Katharena E. Roßfeldt in Germany

The fine landaulette coachwork fitted to this 1934 20/25, chassis GMD3, was built by James Young Ltd of Bromley, Kent.

The famous Yorkshire firm Rippon Bros built the tall, traditional limousine coachwork on this 1936 25/30, chassis GHL18. The high, limousine steering column rake, very evident in this photograph, imposed a 'sit up and beg' driving position on the chauffeur, while chassis intended for more sporting bodies invariably had the low column rake.

This extremely handsome and sporty drophead coupé, which has been owned for many years by well known Rolls-Royce author Lawrence Dalton, was built by Salmons on 1936 25/30 chassis GXN5.

course and it was announced that the British Central Equitable Trust, acting for another firm, had lodged a higher offer for Bentley Motors. It was later revealed that the firm in question was Rolls-Royce Ltd, who paid £125,275 for the assets of Bentley Motors.

In the meantime, the aero business had grown to such an extent that cars had become something of a side-line for Rolls-Royce, even after the scope for sales had been expanded by the acquisition of Bentley Motors Ltd. A new company, Bentley Motors (1931) Ltd, was set up to market Bentley cars, though the first of the Derby Bentleys did not appear until 1933. W. O. Bentley, who had been acquired by Rolls-Royce along with the other

assets, was allowed no direct part in the design of the Derby Bentleys and was at first assigned to Percy Northey at Conduit Street, looking after the demonstration cars. Subsequently he became involved in the road testing of Rolls-Royce and, later, the new Bentley cars, and ultimately became technical adviser to the Managing Director. The first Derby Bentley was the 3½ Litre, which W. O. declared to be the best car ever to bear his name, putting aside any lingering animosity he might have felt towards its makers.

The 3½ Litre used the chassis frame of the abandoned Rolls-Royce 'Peregrine' project, which had been a proposed smaller, lighter and more economical Rolls-Royce car aimed at

keeping sales up during the Depression. Married to a more highly tuned twin SU carburetter version of the contemporary Rolls-Royce 20/25 engine with higher compression ratio and a more sporting camshaft, it formed the basis of 'The Silent Sports Car', as the Bentley was lauded at its introduction.

The Bentley car as built by Rolls-Royce combined the traditional Rolls-Royce attributes of silence, smoothness and refinement with the exceptional performance and sporting handling associated with the Bentley marque. This proved a winning combination and sporting drivers such as Raymond Mays, Eddie Hall, Malcolm Campbell and George Eyston quickly became

A 1937 Bentley 4¼ Litre drophead coupé by Vanden Plas, chassis B104JD.

A Bentley 4¼ Litre H. J. Mulliner 'High Vision' two-door saloon. Note the Perspex panel above the windscreen, the slim chrome-plated side window frames and the very slim windscreen pillars – all designed to provide maximum visibility.

The Derby Bentleys are considerably smaller than even the small-horsepower Rolls-Royce cars, and they were intended to be sporting rather than formal cars. A saloon with division must therefore be regarded as extremely unusual. This Hooper saloon with division was built on 4¼ Litre chassis B142HK for HRH The Duke of Kent. Note the absence of running boards.

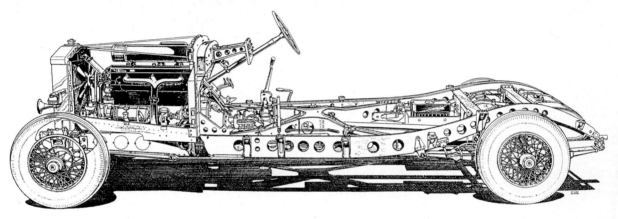

Introduced in 1938, the Wraith was the last of the small-horsepower pre-war Rolls-Royce models. The independent front suspension was similar in design to that of the Wraith's larger stablemate, the Phantom III.

This is an experimental Wraith, chassis 27GVI, later renumbered WXA6 in the production chassis series. The attractive razor-edge saloon coachwork is by Park Ward. This photograph was used in the Wraith sales catalogue.

Another photograph from the Wraith sales catalogue, also showing an experimental Wraith, chassis 24GVI, later renumbered WXA3. The extremely roomy Pullman limousine coachwork is by Park Ward.

converts and found that for fast, fatigue-free, long-distance motoring the Derby Bentley had no peers. Raymond Mays used his for pre-race practice and track familiarisation, often after long drives to the venue.

In 1936 the engine bore was increased to 3½ inches and the small-horsepower Rolls-Royce became the 25/30. The 20/25 had acquired a proprietary Marston radiator in 1933 and the last few of that model had a Borg & Beck clutch. This policy of

what would today be called 'out-sourcing' was further developed on the 25/30, which had a bought-out Stromberg carburetter and SU petrol pumps. The 4,257 cc engine was also adopted for the Bentley, which became the 4¼ Litre. Again, twin SU carburetters, a more sporting camshaft and higher compression ratio transformed the engine for Bentley use.

Whilst motorways in Britain were still 20 years away, fast limited access roads were already being built on the

Continent, notably in Germany and Italy, enabling drivers to cruise at higher speeds for longer periods than was possible on even the best British 'A' roads. The provision of Hall's Metal bearings on the 4¼ Litre helped fit the Bentley for this new development, and the advent of the 1939 'M' series 4¼, with overdrive gearbox and superior engine lubrication system, meant that even more effortless, prolonged high-speed cruising was possible without risk to

A razor-edge 'high vision' saloon by H. J. Mulliner on 1938 Wraith chassis WXA87. Note the slim windscreen pillars and chrome side window frames – both features designed to maximise visibility from inside the car, hence the term 'high vision'.

the engine. Third gear became the direct drive, though the final drive ratio was lowered slightly.

The final development of the pre-war small-horsepower Rolls-Royce came in 1938 with the introduction of the 25/30 hp 'Wraith' – more popularly known simply as the Wraith. In this model the traditional Rolls-Royce attributes of silence and smoothness were developed to a remarkable degree, but the car had put on a considerable amount of weight and in this respect at least lost much of the charm of its ancestor the Twenty. The weight of coachwork in particular had become a cause of considerable concern to the Company.

The chassis of the Wraith was entirely new, with a cruciform bracing rather like that of its larger stablemate, the Phantom III, and of largely welded construction. The most important new feature, however, was the independent front suspension, which was similar to that of the Phantom III. Other than retaining the same bore and stroke (3½ inches by 4½ inches) as the 25/30, the engine was entirely new, with a simplified timing gear train, Hall's Metal big-ends and a new cross-flow cylinder head design derived from the parallel Bentley development.

Though the outbreak of the Second World War stopped production of this very pleasing and satisfactory model, the likelihood is that it would only have remained for a further year or so in any case. The Company was losing money on motor car production and the programme designed to reverse this – development of the Rationalised Range – was already well advanced.

By the close of the 1930s both the 'large' and 'small' Rolls-Royce models had acquired independent front suspension, and the Bentley, being the sporting model of the range, appeared all the more conspicuous for its leaf-sprung front beam axle. It was vital that the Bentley be brought up to date in this respect and not be seen to be lagging behind the contemporary Rolls-Royce models. Thus the final pre-Second World War Bentley was the Mk V, which was the first manifestation of the Rationalised Range of models then under development, with a new design of independent front suspension in a completely new chassis. Only 11 Mk Vs were completed before war curtailed motor car production.

A Continental version of the Mk V, called the 'Corniche', was also under development. An experimental Corniche, which reached the French testing stage, used the 'rationalised' engine with overhead inlet and side exhaust valves, and bolt-on pressed steel wheels. In its specification this car formed the basis of the post-war models, both Bentley and Rolls-Royce, and in its concept it anticipated the post-war Bentley Continental.

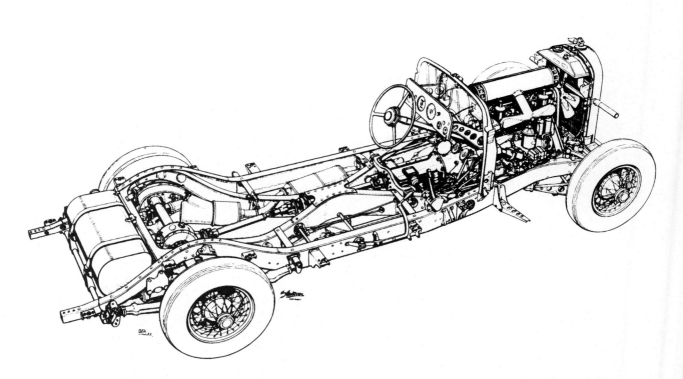

The Bentley Mk V was the first manifestation of the 'Rationalised Range' project and the first Bentley with independent front suspension. Only a handful were completed before the Second World War put an end to chassis production at Derby.

TECHNICAL SPECIFICATIONS

Rolls-Royce 20 hp, 20/25, 25/30, Wraith; Bentley 3½ Litre, 4¼ Litre, Mk V; 1922-1939

Engine

Six cylinders in line. Cast iron crankcase, cylinder block and detachable cylinder head.
Bore 3 inches, stroke 4½ inches, cubic capacity 4,257 cc. Overhead valves, single gear-driven camshaft. Seven-bearing crankshaft. Royce two-jet carburetter.

1929 (20/25), 1933 (Bentley 3½ Litre): Bore 3¼ inches, cubic capacity 3,699 cc.
1933 (Bentley 3½ Litre): Twin SU carburetters.
1934 (20/25): Single-jet expanding carburetter.
1936 (25/30 and Bentley 4¼ Litre), 1938 (Wraith), 1939 (Bentley Mk V): Bore 3½ inches, cubic capacity 4,257 cc; Stromberg downdraught carburetter (25/30 and Wraith); twin SU carburetters (Bentley 4¼ Litre and Mk V).

Chassis

Channel-section frame with tubular cross-members.
Wheelbase 10 ft 9 in (20 hp and early 20/25), 11 ft 0 in (20/25 from 1930 and 25/30), 11 ft 4 in (Wraith), 10 ft 6 in (Bentley 3½ Litre and 4¼ Litre), 10 ft 4 in (Bentley Mk V).

1938 (Wraith): Welded frame with cruciform centre bracing.
1939 (Bentley Mk V): Riveted frame with cruciform centre bracing.

Transmission

Three forward speeds and reverse, centre change. Single dry-plate clutch.
Open propeller shaft.

Fully-floating final drive with spiral bevel gears.

1925: Four-speed gearbox with right-hand gate-type change.
1932: Synchromesh on third and top gears.
1933 (Bentley), 1936 (late 20/25 and 25/30): Hypoid rear axle.
1938 (Wraith), 1939 (Bentley Mk V): Synchromesh on second, third and top gears.

Steering

Worm and nut.
1936 (late 20/25, 25/30), 1938 (Wraith), 1939 (late Bentley 4¼ Litre and Mk V): Cam and roller.

Suspension

Front and rear: semi-elliptic leaf springs protected by leather gaiters, friction dampers.
1928: Rear hydraulic dampers.
1932: Split piston hydraulic shock dampers.
1934: Adjustable hydraulic shock dampers controlled by pump and governor on gearbox with overriding hand control on steering wheel boss.
1938 (Wraith): Independent front suspension by wishbones and horizontal coil springs enclosed in oil-filled casings.
1939 (Bentley Mk V): Independent front suspension by wishbones and coil springs.

Brakes

Footbrake and handbrake operating side by side on rear drums, internal expanding.

1925: Four-wheel brakes with friction disc servo driven by gearbox.
1938 (Wraith), 1939 (Bentley Mk V): Handbrake and footbrake used same shoes in rear drums.

Chassis lubrication system

By oil gun.
1929 (late 20 hp and 20/25): Partially centralised chassis lubrication system introduced, with reservoir

and pump on engine side of dash.
1932: Fully centralised system.

Fuel system

Rear-mounted petrol tank, Autovac feed.

1933 (Bentley), 1936 (25/30): SU dual fuel pump.

Road wheels and tyres

23-inch straight-sided, wire wheels.

1927: 21-inch well-base wire wheels.
1929 (20/25): 19-inch.
1933 (Bentley): 18-inch.
1938 (Wraith), 1939 (late Bentley 4¼ Litre): 17-inch.
1939 (Bentley Mk V): 16-inch.

CHASSIS NUMBERS

Twenty
The number 13 was omitted from all series.

Chassis numbers	Year
40G1-50G0	1922-23
50S1-60S0, 60H1-60H0, 70A1-80A0, 80K1-90K0	1923
GA1-GA81, GF1-GF81	1923/24
GH1-GH81, GAK1-GAK81, GMK1-GMK81, GRK1-GRK84	1924
GDK1-GDK81	1924/25
GLK1-GLK81, GNK1 GNK94, GPK1-GPK81, GSK1-GSK81	1925-26
GCK1-GCK81, GOK1-GOK81, GZK1-GZK81, GUK1-GUK81, GYK1-GYK81	1926
GMJ1-GMJ81, GHJ1-GHJ81, GAJ1-GAJ81, GRJ1-GRJ81, GUJ1-GUJ81	1927
GXL1-GXL81, GYL1-GYL81, GWL1-GWL41	1927-28
GBM1-GBM81, GKM1-GKM81, GTM1-GTM41	1928
GFN1-GFN81, GLN1-GLN81, GEN1-GEN81	1928-29
GVO1-GVO81, GXO1-GXO10	1929

Total: 2,940 cars.

20/25

The number 13 was omitted from all series.

Chassis numbers	Year
GXO11-GXO111	1929
GGP1-GGP81, GDP1-GDP81, GWP1-GWP41	1929-30
GLR1-GLR81, GSR1-GSR81, GTR1-GTR41	1930
GNS1-GNS81, GOS1-GOS81, GPS1-GPS41	1930-31
GFT1-GFT81, GBT1-GBT81, GKT1-GKT41	1931-32
GAU1-GAU81, GMU1-GMU81, GZU1-GZU41	1932
GHW1-GHW81, GRW1-GRW81, GAW1-GAW41	1932-33
GEX1-GEX81, GWX1-GWX81, GDX1-GDX41	1933
GSY1-GSY101	1933
GLZ1-GLZ81, GTZ1-GTZ81, GYZ1-GYZ41	1933
GBA1-GBA81, GGA1-GGA81, GHA1-GHA41	1933
GXB1-GXB81, GUB1-GUB81, GLB1-GLB41	1933-34
GNC1-GNC81, GRC1-GRC81, GKC1-GKC41	1934
GED1-GED81, GMD1-GMD81, GYD1-GYD41	1934
GAE1-GAE81, GWE1-GWE81, GFE1-GFE41	1934
GAF1-GAF81, GSF1-GSF81, GRF1-GRF41	1934-35
GLG1-GLG81, GPG1-GPG81, GHG1-GHG41	1935
GYH1-GYH81, GOH1-GOH81, GEH1-GEH41	1935
GBJ1-GBJ81, GLJ1-GLJ81, GCJ1-GCJ41	1935
GXK1-GXK81, GBK1-GBK81, GTK1-GTK53	1935-36

Total: 3,827 cars.

Bentley 3½ Litre

Chassis sub-series starting with 1 use odd numbers only, omitting 13. Those starting with 2 use even numbers only.

Chassis numbers	Year
B1AE-B203AE, B2AH-B198AH	1933-34
B1BL-B201BL, B2BN-B99BN	1933-34
B2CR-B200CR, B1CW-B203CW	1933-34
B2DG-B200DG, B1DK-B199DK	1935
B2EF-B200EF, B1EJ-B203EJ	1935
B2FB-B200FB, B1FC-B159FC	1935

Total: 1,191 cars.

25/30

The number 13 was omitted from all series.

Chassis number	Year
GUL1-GUL81, GTL1-GTL81, GHL1-GHL41	1936-37
GRM1-GRM81, GXM1-GXM81, GGM1-GGM41	1936-37
GAN1-GAN81, GWN1-GWN81, GUN1-GUN41	1936-37
GRO1-GRO81, GHO1-GHO81, GMO1-GMO81	1937
GRP1-GRP81, GMP1-GMP81, GLP1-GLP41	1937
GAR1-GAR81, GGR1-GGR81, GZR1-GZR41	1937-38

Total: 1,240 cars.

Bentley 4¼ Litre

Chassis sub-series starting with 1 use odd numbers only, omitting 13. Those starting with 2 use even numbers only.

Chassis numbers	Year
B2GA-B260GA, B1GP-B203GP	1936
B2HK-B200HK, B1HM-B203HM	1936
B2JD-B200JD, B1JY-B203JY	1937
B2KT-B200KT, B1KU-B203KU	1937
B2LS-B204LS, B1LE-B203LE	1938
B2MR-B200MR, B1MX-B205MX	1939

Total: 1,233 cars.

Wraith

The number 13 was omitted from all series.

Chassis numbers	Year
WXA1-WXA109	1938-39
WRB1-WRB81, WMB1-WMB81, WLB1-WLB41	1938-39
WHC1-WHC81, WEC1-WEC81, WKC1-WKC25	1939

Total: 491 cars.

Bentley Mk V

Even numbers only.

Chassis numbers	Year
B10AW-B24AW	1939
B30AW-B34AW	1939

Not completed: B2AW-B8AW, B26AW, B28AW, B36AW. Chassis B38AW used to rebuild accident-damaged B22AW.

Total completed: 11 cars.

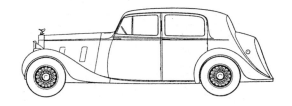

Chapter Four

The pre-war Phantoms

The 40/50 hp was soon to catch up with its smaller stablemate the 20 hp in respect of its engine, with the introduction of the New Phantom (now mostly known by its retrospective model designation Phantom I) in 1925. This model had a new 7.7 litre overhead valve six-cylinder engine, though most of the chassis details remained unchanged from the Silver Ghost, which remained in production for a short time alongside the new model.

The bore was reduced from 4½ inches to 4¼ inches, providing owners with a £6 per year tax saving. The fact that the stroke had been lengthened from 4¾ inches to 5½ inches and that the new car's power output was certainly not diminished underlines the absurdity of the so-called 'horsepower tax', which took into account the bore but ignored the stroke. The New Phantom was fitted, like the Twenty, with a disc-type clutch and a set of radiator shutters. The latter, unlike those of the Twenty, were vertical.

The first entirely new 40/50 hp chassis came in 1929 when the Phantom II was announced. With its low-slung chassis, radiator set well back behind the front axle, very long bonnet and steering wheel more than half way back in the wheelbase, the Phantom II was a superbly proportioned motor car. This new chassis enabled the coachbuilders to progress from basically carriage-like coachwork to the much sleeker designs of the 1930s.

In its layout the Phantom II chassis was essentially a scaled-up Twenty. The gearbox was in unit with the engine, the propeller shaft was open and the rear axle was located by its semi-elliptic springs. The 40/50 hp model had therefore caught up with its smaller stablemate in chassis design as well as engine.

It was during the production run of the Phantom II, on 22 April 1933, that Sir Henry Royce, who had been knighted in 1931, died. At around the same time the enamel in the famous radiator badge was changed from red to black, and this inevitably passed into mythology as a mark of respect for Royce. Other reasons for the change have been suggested, such as a desire to avoid the colour of Bolshevism and a need to avoid clashing with the colours then being applied to coachwork, but whatever the reason it is known that Royce himself approved the change before his death, so the mark of respect myth can be safely discounted.

The Phantom II underwent continuous development during its six-year production run, acquiring such modern features as thermostatically operated radiator shutters and one-shot chassis lubrication in 1931, and synchromesh (at first on third and top gears only) in 1932. A Continental version, with more sporting performance and typically a shorter wheelbase chassis, was introduced in 1930, and is much sought after today.

By this time the Company was heavily involved in aero engine production, enjoying considerable success in that field and basking in the glories of achievements such as the 1929 and '31 Schneider Trophy wins. The Phantom III motor car, introduced in 1936, reflected aero practice in its complex V-12 engine.

The Phantom III engine was an aluminium alloy 60-degree V-12 with the same bore and stroke, 3¼ by 4½

A 1926 Phantom I open drive limousine, or brougham, by Clark of Wolverhampton, chassis 76TC. The original owner of this extraordinary car was a collector of fine French furniture and no expense was spared in decorating and furnishing the rear compartment of the car in the manner to which he was accustomed at home. The upholstery was Aubusson petit-point, which cost over £600, and the ceiling was painted by a French artist.

A 1928 Phantom I with enclosed drive limousine coachwork by Park Ward, chassis 52AL.

A Phantom I with typical touring coachwork of the period, probably by Barker.

The Weymann system was a lightweight method of coachwork construction using squeak-proof timber framing and weather-proof fabric outer covering in place of the usual aluminium. This is a Weymann fabric saloon by H. J. Mulliner on 1929 Phantom I chassis 12KR.

*Chassis 81CL, with sedanca de ville coachwork by Hooper, was completed early in 1929 for the Vienna Motor Show.
The F2B series, lettered 'CL', was the first to have the aluminium cylinder head. Note the flush-fitting radiator shutters
of these late Phantom Is. The year 1929 was the last to see New Phantom production at Derby, but construction of the
American version continued at Springfield, Massachusetts, for a further two years.*

*In the garden of Royce's summer
home, 'Elmstead' at West Wittering,
Sussex, 8 September 1929. Royce is
at the centre on the far side of the
table. With him, clockwise from him
around the table, are A. G. Elliott,
Bernard Day (patting Royce's
labrador Rajah), W. G. Hardy, R. L.
Marmont, Charles Jenner, nurse
Ethel Aubin and Ivan Evernden,
celebrating the Schneider Trophy
victory. Drawings, designs, ideas and
even complete experimental cars
circulated freely between here (or in
winter Royce's home at Le Canadel in
the south of France) and the Derby
works.*

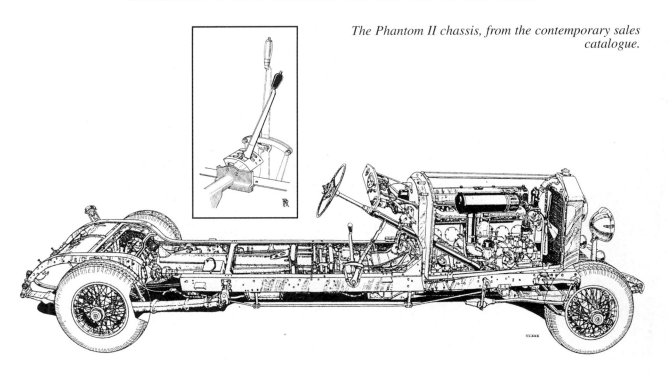

The Phantom II chassis, from the contemporary sales catalogue.

Royce in France with 21EX, an experimental Phantom II and the first British Rolls-Royce with left-hand drive. With Royce are nurse Aubin, Ernest Hives and A. G. Elliott. Hives (later Lord Hives) started with Rolls-Royce in 1908 as a car tester, having previously worked for C. S. Rolls, eventually rising to Managing Director. Elliott was Chief Engineer from 1937 and became joint Managing Director (with Hives) in 1945.

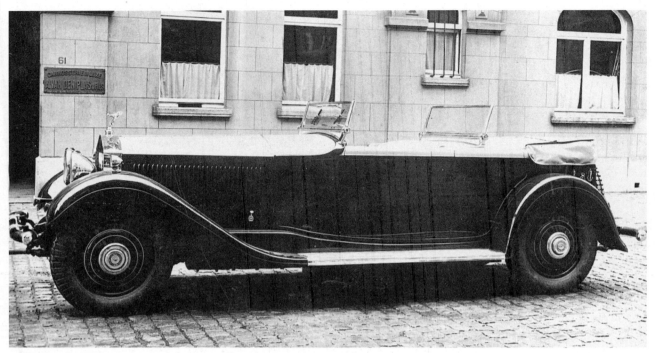

1930 Phantom II chassis 43GX with rakish tourer coachwork by Van Den Plas (Brussels), outside whose offices the photograph was taken. Note the second windscreen for the rear seat passengers.

1931 Phantom II chassis 9JS, Barker sedanca de ville. This car was made famous by the MGM film 'The Yellow Rolls-Royce'.

The three-position drophead coupe in this illustration from the Phantom II sales catalogue is characteristic of the type of coachwork for which the Continental chassis was intended

1934 Phantom II chassis 16SK, a drophead coupé by Chapron of Paris, photographed by Thomas T. Solley who owned and restored it in the 1980s.

The Phantom III engine – the legendary V-12 – and chassis reproduced from the sales catalogue for that model.

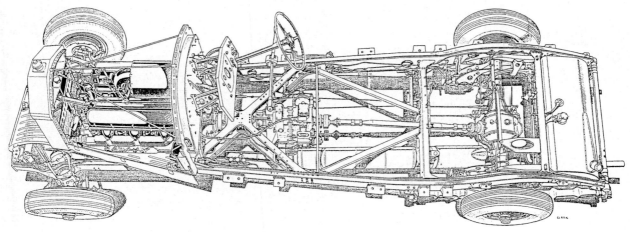

1937 Phantom III chassis 3CP200, with close-coupled sedanca de ville coachwork by Hooper. The two-tone finish to the wings, the spats on the rear wings and the chrome embellishments are all unusual features

The introduction of the Phantom III in 1936 corresponded with the emergence of 'razor-edge' coachwork, of which the H.J. Mulliner sports saloon on chassis 3CP108 (above) is typical. More exceptional, perhaps, is the same coachbuilder's touring limousine on chassis 3DL184 (below), which displays the very slim windscreen pillars, chrome-plated side window surrounds, chrome waistline 'spear' and wing swagelines, all of which contributed to H.J. Mulliner's distinctive 'look', which was carried forward into the post-war period.

A superb rakish sedanca de ville design by Gurney Nutting on 1936 Phantom III chassis 3AZ168.

For the Phantom III Gurney Nutting developed their three-position drophead coupé design seen on the Phantom II on page 49 (and in the colour section). This is 1936 Phantom III chassis 3AZ158

inches, as the contemporary 20/25 hp. Carburation was to have been by four downdraught carburetters, and the earliest published catalogues showed and described this arrangement. In the event, however, all production Phantom IIIs had a single dual-choke Stromberg carburetter mounted in the centre of the vee. The carburetter and its air silencer, the cylinder heads and the valve rocker covers were beautifully finished in the traditional Rolls-Royce black stove enamel. The rocker covers, for the first time, did not bear their maker's name but were elegantly plain and attached by no fewer than 14 dome-nuts, like fine stitching. With its twin distributors at the front of the engine and finned exhaust manifolds, this all made for a very impressive under-bonnet appearance. Performance was equally impressive. When not burdened by large, heavy coachwork, the last of these cars could reach a genuine 100 mph, with silent turbine-like acceleration and wonderful top-gear flexibility.

The Phantom III was the first Rolls-Royce with independent front suspension. Maurice Olley, who had moved from Rolls-Royce to Cadillac in 1930, after the closure of the Springfield factory of which he was Chief Engineer, helped facilitate good relations between Derby and Detroit.

Olley worked on suspension design and developed the General Motors 'knee-action' system of i.f.s., which was adopted for the Phantom III, being considered the best and most suitable system available after testing several of the best American and European i.f.s.-equipped cars. As fitted to the Phantom III it was superbly made, with semi-trailing wishbones and horizontal coil springs enclosed, with their shock dampers, in oil-filled housings. The rear suspension, by semi-elliptic springs, appeared more conventional. Other manufacturers, however, did not feel the need to grind painstakingly each leaf to a perfect fit with its neighbour, feed the springs with oil from the one-shot system and enclose them in beautifully made leather gaiters as did Rolls-Royce.

The chassis frame was entirely new, being much stiffer than that of its predecessor, with a large cruciform bracing in the middle. The engine and radiator were mounted much further forward in the frame and, curiously, the separate gearbox layout was reverted to, with a fabric joint in the clutch to gearbox shaft. The forward mounting of the engine allowed the wheelbase to come down to 11 ft 10 in without sacrificing space for coachwork.

Unfortunately some of the advanced features of the Phantom III caused trouble, particularly after long periods of wartime storage. The hydraulic tappets were ahead of their time and more than the oils and oil filters of the day could cope with unless the recommended oil changing periods were strictly adhered to. The oil/water heat exchanger also gave trouble and the aluminium blocks corroded around the 'wet' cylinder liners causing leaks and over-heating.

The final ('D' series) cars received solid tappets and Hall's Metal big-end bearings. A new four-port cylinder head increased the power output and the oil cooler was deleted. The last few cars, the most desirable of all, had an overdrive gearbox for fast, low-rpm cruising.

Some enthusiasts regard the Phantom III as the finest motor car of all time. A few more years of customary Rolls-Royce development could well have turned this from opinion into solid fact, and it would be easy to assume that but for the outbreak of war this would actually have occurred. In truth, however, it is probable that the Phantom III would have been discontinued in any case at the end of 1940. The Phantom III was far too expensive to make and the 'Rationalised Range' was waiting in the wings.

TECHNICAL SPECIFICATIONS

Phantom I, II and III

PHANTOM I

As late four-wheel brake Silver Ghost, *except:*

Engine

Detachable cast iron cylinder head. Bore 4¼ inches, stroke 5½ inches, cubic capacity 7,668 cc. Overhead valves with single camshaft. Seven-bearing crankshaft. Royce two-jet carburetter.

1928: Aluminium alloy cylinder head; side-by-side rear brakes.

Springfield model left-hand drive with centre gear change.

CHASSIS NUMBERS

Phantom I

The number 13 was omitted.

Chassis numbers	Year
1MC-122MC, 1RC-125RC, 1HC-122HC	1925
1LC-131LC, 1SC-121SC, 1DC-121DC	1926
1TC-121TC, 1YC-123YC, 1NC-131NC	1926-27
1EF-101EF, 1LF-101LF, 1RF-101RF, 1UF-101UF	1927
1EH-101EH, 1FH-101FH	1928
1AL-101AL, 1CL-101CL	1928-29
1WR-131WR, 1KR-131KR, 1OR-90OR	1928-29

Springfield Phantom I

Chassis numbers	Year
S400FL-S465FL	1926
S66PM-S200PM, S201RM-S300RM, S301FM-S400FM	1927
S101RP-S200RP, S201FP-S300FP, S301KP-S400KP	1928
S101FR-S200FR	1928-29
S201KR-S300KR, S301LR-S400LR	1929
S401MR-S500MR	1930
S101PR-S241PR	1930-31

Total: 2,212 Derby Phantom I, 1,241 Springfield Phantom I.

PHANTOM II

Engine

Six cylinders in line, cast in two blocks of three. Aluminium alloy crankcase and cylinder head. Bore 4¼ inches, stroke 5½ inches, cubic capacity 7,668 cc. Overhead valves with single camshaft. Seven-bearing crankshaft. Royce two-jet carburetter.

1933: Single-jet semi-expanding carburetter.

Chassis

Channel-section frame with tubular cross-members.
Overall length 17 ft 2 in (long), 16 ft 8 in (short).
Wheelbase 12 ft 6 in (long), 12 ft 0 in (short).

Transmission

Four forward speeds and reverse, right-hand gate change. Single dry-plate clutch. Centre change on AMS and AJS series left-hand-drive cars. Open propeller shaft.
Fully floating final drive with hypoid bevel gears.

1933: Synchromesh on third and top gears.
1935: Synchromesh on second gear.

Steering

Worm and nut.

Suspension

Front and rear: semi-elliptic leaf springs protected by leather gaiters, friction dampers.

1933: Adjustable hydraulic shock dampers controlled by pump and governor on gearbox with overriding hand control on steering wheel boss.

Brakes

Four-wheel brakes with friction disc servo driven by gearbox. Handbrake on separate shoes in rear drums.

Chassis lubrication system

Partially centralised system, with reservoir and pump on engine side of dash; remainder by oil gun.

1931: Complete centralised system.

Fuel system

Rear-mounted petrol tank; feed by Autovac and engine-driven vacuum pump.

Road wheels and tyres

21-inch well-base wire wheels.

1930: 20-inch.
1933: 19-inch.

CHASSIS NUMBERS

Phantom II

The number 13 was omitted.

Chassis numbers	Year
1WJ-133WJ, 1XJ-204XJ	1929-30
1GN-202GN, 1GY-205GY	1930
1GX-68GX	1931
1JS-84JS, 2MS-170MS	1931-32
201AJS-303AJS, 201AMS-224AMS	1931-34
2MY-190MY, 3MW-107MW	1933
2PY-206PY, 3RY-211RY	1933-34
2SK-196SK	1934
1TA-201TA	1934-35
2UK-82UK	1935
84UK	1936

Total: 1,768 cars.

PHANTOM III

Engine

Twelve cylinders in 60-degree V formation. Aluminium alloy monobloc crankcase and cylinder block. Aluminium alloy cylinder heads. Bore 3¼ inches, stroke 4½ inches, cubic capacity 7,340 cc. Overhead valves with single camshaft. Seven-bearing crankshaft. Stromberg dual-choke downdraught carburetter.

Chassis

Channel-section frame with cruciform centre-bracing. Overall length 15 ft 11 in. Wheelbase 11 ft 10 in.

Transmission

Four forward speeds and reverse, right-hand gate change. Single dry-plate clutch. Synchromesh on second, third and top gears. Open propeller shaft. Fully floating final drive with hypoid bevel gears.

1938: Overdrive top gear.

Steering

Cam and roller.

Suspension

Front: independent by wishbones and horizontal coil springs enclosed in oil-filled casings.
Rear: semi-elliptic leaf springs protected by leather gaiters, adjustable hydraulic shock dampers controlled by pump and governor on gearbox with overriding hand control on steering wheel boss.

Brakes

Four-wheel brakes with friction disc servo driven by gearbox. Handbrake operating on rear wheels.

Chassis lubrication system

Centralised system, with reservoir and pump on engine side of dash.

Fuel system

Rear-mounted petrol tank; twin SU electric fuel pump.

Road wheels and tyres

18-inch well-base wire wheels.

CHASSIS NUMBERS

Phantom III

Chassis sub-series starting with 1 use odd numbers only, with the addition of 3AX34, 3AX36, 3CM108 and 3CM112, and omitting 13 and 113. Those starting with 2 use even numbers only, with the addition of 3AZ43, 3AX47 and 3DH9.

Chassis numbers	Year
3AZ20-3AZ238, 3AX1-3AX207	1936
3BU2-3BU200, 3BT1-3BT203	1936-37
3CP2-3CP200, 3CM1-3CM203	1937-38
3DL2-3DL200, 3DH1-3DH9	1938-39

Total: 717 cars, plus 10 experimental cars, many of which were upgraded to production specification and sold.

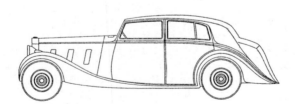

Chapter Five

Rationalisation
and the post-war cars

In 1937 a decision was reached by the Rolls-Royce Ltd Board to create a separate Chassis Division responsible for its own contribution to Company profitability. This meant a re-think of the way cars had been built virtually regardless of cost with few parts in common between models. The 'Rationalised Range' of cars was conceived, with a common chassis design (in varying lengths) and common drive-train. Though there were to be both six- and eight-cylinder engines, and potentially even a four-cylinder, most of the moving parts were common to all engines. Thus great savings could be made without in any way compromising quality. Ironically, in a sense this represented a reversion to pre-1907 design philosophy, before the comprehensive range of cars then offered was replaced by a single model, the Silver Ghost.

The first manifestation of the rationalisation policy was the Bentley Mk V, only 11 examples of which were completed before the Second World War interrupted car production. The Mk V chassis incorporated most of the rationalisation scheme features,

with the notable exception of the engine, which was an overhead valve unit similar to that of the Wraith but with twin SU carburetters as was customary for Bentleys. Had the war not intervened, for 1940 this model would have received the new engine, the most important distinguishing feature of which was an overhead inlet, side exhaust valve arrangement (another feature shared with the pre-1907 range). The Phantom III and Wraith would have been discontinued in favour of Rationalised models with in-line eight- and six-cylinder engines respectively. In the event, however, the Rationalised Range had to await the end of the war and resumption of car production.

When motor car production was resumed in 1946 the Car Division, as it was now called, was geographically separated from the Aero Engine Division. When the Chassis Division had first been created before the war consideration had been given to moving it out of Derby into its own factory at Burton-on-Trent. In the event, however, this move did not take place, and after the war the Division was moved into the Crewe

factory, which had been purpose-built for the production of Merlin aircraft engines for the war effort. Aero engine production at Crewe was almost at an end, leaving available a superbly equipped new factory and a highly skilled workforce. Unlike most other British manufacturers, who were obliged to reintroduce barely disguised versions of their pre-war models, Rolls-Royce had its completely new range of cars ready for production with all the design spade-work completed before the war.

The use of 'bought-out' proprietary engine ancillaries had begun on the Springfield Silver Ghost, though little other than the magneto had been bought out for the British Silver Ghost. The influence of Henry Royce remained strong at Derby, and with his electrical engineering background he could see little reason to purchase such electrical items when they could be made to carefully controlled standards in the Company's own factory.

Carburetters too were designed and manufactured by Rolls-Royce. The first Rolls-Royce products to have

Just before the Second World War the Experimental Department based at Belper, near Derby, installed the 5.3-litre in-line eight-cylinder version of the range of engines then under development for the 'Rationalised Range' of cars into a Bentley V chassis. This was experimental chassis 11BV, fitted with Park Ward saloon coachwork and called 'Comet' – although its performance gave rise to the colourfully descriptive but unofficial name 'Scalded Cat'. In the event, the eight-cylinder rationalised engine was used only in the very limited production Phantom IV, though a military/commercial version, the B.80, was made in large numbers.

The Crewe factory of Rolls-Royce Ltd was opened in 1938, having been purpose-built for the production of Merlin aero engines in preparation for the inevitability of the Second World War. After the war motor car production was moved to Crewe to take advantage of a fine new factory and a highly skilled workforce.

The original 10-foot wheelbase Bentley Mk VI chassis used the shorter of the two rationalised frames introduced immediately after the war. The Silver Wraith chassis was similar, but 7 inches longer in its original short wheelbase guise, and was fitted exclusively with individual coachwork, no standard steel saloon being available for that chassis. The Silver Dawn chassis, introduced in 1949, was identical to that of the Bentley Mk VI except that it used the Silver Wraith-type engine, with single carburetter.

The Bentley Mk VI standard steel saloon was the first complete car to be manufactured by Rolls-Royce Ltd. Previously, only chassis were built and coachwork was constructed and fitted by outside coachbuilders. This is a 1952 car; earlier standard steel saloons lacked the chrome waistline embellisher strip. The side scuttle ventilators shown here were introduced in 1951, a single scuttle-top vent being fitted previously.

bought-out carburetters were the first Derby-built Bentley cars, introduced just after Royce's death, which, like their forerunners built by the old Bentley Motors Ltd, had SU carburetters. In 1936 the Phantom III appeared with a Stromberg carburetter, and the 25/30 hp and 1938 Wraith followed suit. Such bought-out components as SU electric petrol pumps also appeared on these models. For the Rationalised Range this policy was to be extended to the fitting of Lucas Special Equipment dynamos, starters and other electrical components.

The rationalised engine was a cast iron monobloc unit, ie with the cylinder block and crankcase cast as a single unit, with side exhaust valves operated directly from the camshaft. The aluminium alloy cylinder head carried the overhead inlet valves, which were operated through pushrods and rockers. It will be recalled that this overhead inlet, side exhaust valve ('F'-head) arrangement had been used on Royce's original range of engines more than 30 years before. It allowed larger valves and freer gas flow for better efficiency and more power without the need to use noisier means to these ends such as overhead camshafts.

For the first time on a Rolls-Royce engine, belt drive was used for the water pump and dynamo, the fan being attached to the water pump shaft. Carburation was by a dual-choke downdraught Stromberg carburetter for the Rolls-Royce cars and twin SUs on the Bentley.

Realising that the surviving coachbuilders would be hard pressed to provide traditional coachwork for the volume of car production envisaged for the brave new world of the post-war period, the Company had embarked on an ambitious new programme to build complete cars rather than only chassis as before. The steel body shells were supplied by the Pressed Steel Company of Oxford and fitted to the chassis, assembled, painted, trimmed and finished at the Crewe factory. At first only the Bentley model, the Mk VI, was involved, and the Rolls-Royce Silver

Wraith was always offered with traditional coachbuilt bodies only.

The Standard Steel Saloons found ready acceptance and only one flaw in the whole concept prevents its being regarded as a complete success. This was the unfortunate fact that the timing of the decision to use pressed steel bodies coincided with the period in which the quality of sheet steel was at its lowest, and many cars succumbed to rust. However, to keep this in perspective, the fact that a much larger proportion of early post-war standard steel saloons have survived in good condition than could be claimed by even their nearest rivals perhaps demonstrates that the problem was not as serious as the marques' detractors would have us believe.

In the early post-war period, with Britain recovering from the enormous damage wrought upon her economy and infrastructure by the war, export earnings were vital. By far the biggest potential export market was the United States, the country to which the bulk of Britain's post-war debt was owed. One thing that quickly became clear was that the most acceptable form of coachwork in America was the standard steel saloon, which was not available on the only Rolls-Royce model offered, the Silver Wraith. It was also true that American buyers wanted their Rolls-Royce to be a Rolls-Royce and not a Bentley – a marque that was much less well known in the United States. For obvious reasons it was also desirable that any car offered for sale in North America should be left-hand drive, whereas the early post-war

The Silver Dawn was introduced in 1949 to satisfy export market requirements for a Rolls-Royce standard steel saloon. The twin fog lamps and heavier export-type bumpers as seen here were standard on this model. Again, this is a 1952 car.

Inside, the Silver Dawn differed from the Bentley Mk VI only in its fascia, which was laid out like that of the Silver Wraith, with separate gauges grouped around a central speedometer and the ignition/lighting 'switchbox' in front of the driver beside the steering column. The Silver Dawn's export markets often called for left-hand drive; such cars had the steering column gear change while right-hand-drive cars had the conventional (for Rolls-Royce) right-hand gate-type gear change.

The early post-war work of H. J.
Mulliner included this handsome six-
light saloon on the Bentley Mk VI
chassis. Unlike the standard steel
saloon, the doors were hinged on their
outer edges and the door window
frames are the slim chromium-plated
type pioneered by Mulliners before the
war for the 'High Vision' coachwork.
The opening panels of the bonnet,
boot and spare wheel compartment
were standard steel saloon
components supplied by Crewe.

The earliest post-war designs of
James Young Ltd resembled, both in
silhouette and details, the last of
their pre-war coachwork, and this
photograph makes an interesting
comparison with that of the Wraith
seen in the colour section. A post-war
change was the sweeping of the front
wings across the doors, rather than
under them, with concealed running
boards. The slim chromium-plated
door window frames and razor-edge
styling with crisp swage lines are
among the features that set this
coachbuilt car apart from the Mk VI
standard steel saloon. Note the early,
rearward-leaning 'winged-B' mascot.

Drophead coupe coachwork had
enjoyed considerable popularity on
the pre-war Bentley chassis, and
after the war Rolls-Royce realised
that there would continue to be a
demand for such cars. Some
coachbuilders utilised standard steel
saloon body panels in their special
coachwork. Here Park Ward & Co
has incorporated the standard steel
front wings into its stylish drophead
coupe on a Bentley Mk VI chassis.

Freestone & Webb's coachbuilt
offering on the Bentley Mk VI chassis
was notably more massive looking
than the standard steel saloon. All
doors of this six-light saloon were
hinged at the rear and the front
wings swept under the doors to form
external running boards.

With its external running boards and traditional lines, Park Ward's early post-war saloon coachwork for the Silver Wraith would not have looked out of place on a pre-war Wraith chassis. Rather staid and upright, but somehow not unattractive.

Again we see that the earliest post-war work of James Young Ltd had strong links with the last of that company's pre-war designs, both in silhouette and styling details. The front wing sweeping across the door panels to conceal the running boards was, however, a new styling feature for the post-war period. Note the very slim windscreen pillars of this 1947 Silver Wraith saloon.

Also displaying strong links with its pre-war work, Freestone & Webb's early post-war bodies featured angular-section wings with exposed running boards and all doors hinged on their rear edges, a basic concept unchanged from that builder's razor-edge coachwork on the Wraith and Phantom III chassis.

Again we see an obvious link with the best of the coachbuilder's pre-war work, in this instance H. J. Mulliner, while nonetheless being all new. Note the low roofline and the slim, chromium-plated brass door window frames.

The 'kneeling' Spirit of Ecstasy mascot had been introduced as an option in 1934 to suit the low-slung coachwork then being introduced. A considerable number of Phantom IIIs were so fitted, but it did not become really popular until the advent of the Wraith in 1938. After the Second World War it became the standard mascot for the Silver Wraith, Silver Dawn and Phantom IV.

Hooper introduced a distinctive cut to the rear quarter-light of its post-war cars. This is the popular 'Teviot', as illustrated in the 1948 Silver Wraith sales catalogue.

The coachbuilding firms Gurney Nutting and James Young were both owned by Jack Barclay Ltd. In the early post-war period the Gurney Nutting name was applied to a small series of Silver Wraith drophead coupés before that famous coachbuilding name faded into obscurity.

A post-war specialty of H. J. Mulliner & Co was the sedanca de ville. Several designs were offered on the early short wheelbase Silver Wraith chassis, of which this is the earliest – in fact, this is the first production Silver Wraith, chassis WTA1. Note the rear-hinged doors and partially exposed running boards.

Rolls-Royce and Bentley cars, like the late pre-war cars, had only been available in right-hand drive.

In response to all this, in 1949 the standard steel saloon concept was extended to the Rolls-Royce car in the shape of a new model, the Silver Dawn. Actually this was not so much a new model as a clever new configuration of existing ones, in that the 120-inch wheelbase chassis, 16-inch wheels and standard steel saloon coachwork of the Bentley Mk VI were combined with the engine of the Silver Wraith, which was in any case the same as that of the Bentley except for its single Stromberg carburetter. Consideration was given to re-tooling the body with an angular shape to the scuttle to match the Rolls-Royce radiator shape. In the event, however, the Car Division balked at the cost of this (about £100,000) and opted instead for a bonnet that changed in shape to accommodate the transition from Rolls-Royce radiator at the front to Bentley scuttle at the rear, allowing the same body shell, with different bonnets, to be used for both models. At the same time all models became available in left-hand drive, with the gear change lever on the steering column in accordance with contemporary American practice.

At the beginning of 1952 a long wheelbase variant of the Silver Wraith was offered. The additional 6 inches of length in this chassis allowed the coachbuilders to build roomier saloon coachwork and limousines with really huge rear compartments with room for usable occasional seats. Once it became available the long wheelbase chassis accounted for most Silver Wraith orders, so the original 127-inch wheelbase chassis was discontinued at the end of the following year.

By 1950 the sweeping of the front wings across the doors to meet the rear wings had become the norm on coachbuilt bodies. Here James Young's four-door saloon in the first picture (left) displays this feature.
A specialist line of James Young Ltd at the time was the 'saloon coupe'. Several designs were produced, of which that in the second picture is a two-door variant of the saloon. On both of these Bentley Mk VIs, note the chrome waist moulding incorporating distinctive door handles with square push-buttons, and the coachbuilder's special bumpers.

Rolls-Royce and Bentley cars in colour

This surviving Light Twenty 26350 has replica TT coachwork built in 1953 when the car was restored by renowned restorer Stanley Sears. It is now owned by UK enthusiast John Kennedy. Inset: The C. S. Rolls & Co plate on the dashboard of the Light Twenty and the Rolls-Royce Ltd maker's plate on the trembler coil box, both bearing the chassis number. The Rolls-Royce plates, of course, only came into use after the formation of the Company in March 1906.

There is no doubt that Royce's masterpiece was the 40/50 hp model, the first examples of which were turned out from Cooke Street in time for a chassis to be exhibited at the 1906 Olympia Motor Show. For the following year's show the 12th 40/50 chassis, 60551, was fitted by Barker & Co with magnificent tourer coachwork, painted in aluminium paint with all fittings silver-plated. This car wore (and still wears) a name-plate bearing the name 'The Silver Ghost', which much later became the type name for the 40/50 hp model. 60551 distinguished itself as a Company demonstration car and was re-acquired by the Company in 1948 when it was fortuitously taken as part exchange on a new Bentley Mk VI. It is still owned by Rolls-Royce Motor Cars Ltd today and remains a powerful publicity tool.

A 1910 Silver Ghost, chassis 1388, restored by South Australian enthusiast the late Laurie Vinall.

1925 Springfield Silver Ghost chassis S128MK, owned by US enthusiast Roger Morrison. The fine American-built coachwork is a Salamanca by Rolls-Royce Custom Coach Works, a Rolls-Royce subsidiary set up to arrange the manufacture of a standard range of coachwork for the Springfield cars.

Many Springfield Silver Ghosts, particularly those with formal coachwork, remained unsold after the 1929 crash. To widen their appeal to secure the sale of both new and used Silver Ghosts, some were re-bodied with sporting coachwork. This 1925 Springfield Silver Ghost, chassis S168MK, was re-bodied in 1931 with this 'Playboy' roadster body, a popular sporting style also fitted to the Springfield Phantom I. The car is seen here on 'Alpine 93' – the 1993 re-enactment of the 1913 Austrian Alpine Trials – in the ownership of Frank and Katherine Miller (USA).

This 1926 Twenty, chassis GYK47, has been owned by Australian 20 hp devotee Terry Bruce since 1964. The saloon-limousine coachwork is by Park Ward.

67

The specification of the final ('M' series) 4¼ Litre Bentleys included an overdrive gearbox for fast, low-rpm cruising. This Vanden Plas four-light drophead coupé on chassis B42MR was exhibited on the Vanden Plas stand at the 1938 London Motor Show – the last before the Second World War.

Perhaps some of the most beautiful and elegant Wraiths were the James Young saloon coupés. Note the ultra-slim windscreen pillars. The off-side rear quarter window appears smaller than its fellow on the near-side because the purdah glass shade has been slid forward. Only three bodies to this design were built, of which this is the last, on chassis WHC47.

The 1926 New Phantom, or Phantom I as it was called after the introduction of the Phantom II. This is chassis 30TC, fitted with Barker cabriolet de ville coachwork.

1929 Phantom I chassis 50OR, of the final series, with Hooper landaulette de ville coachwork (ie the roof over both the front and rear seats can be opened). This car was delivered new to an Australian customer and was converted to an ambulance during the Second World War. It was acquired in 1960 by James Kelso of Sydney, whose determination to return it to original condition resulted some 35 years later in the magnificent motor car seen in this photograph.

1930 Phantom II chassis 143GN with Hooper 'allweather' coachwork – ie a fully opening car like a tourer but with wind-up glass side windows rather than celluloid side-screens. Note the distinctive Hooper patent signal window which allowed the driver to give the regulation hand signals without opening the window.

The Phantom II Continental chassis was designed mainly with sporting coachwork in mind, of which this Park Ward sports saloon on 1934 chassis 24SK, with the author at the wheel, may be regarded as typical.

The Phantom II's very long bonnet, which began aft of the front axle and continued about half-way back in the wheelbase, together with the shorter wheelbase normally used for the Continental chassis, made for superb proportions. Nowhere is this more obvious than in the Gurney Nutting three-position drophead coupé. This example, on chassis 201RY, was once owned by Ray Gentile, author of The Rolls-Royce Phantom II Continental.

1933 Phantom II Continental chassis 42PY. The amazingly styled coupé coachwork is by Freestone & Webb. Note the helmet wings, rear-mounted spare wheel and absence of running boards. This spectacular Rolls-Royce is owned by US enthusiasts David and Jill Scheibel.

The Phantom II was never built at the American factory at Springfield. However, two series of left-hand-drive chassis, the AJS and AMS series, were built with the US market mainly in mind. This is 1931 chassis 250AJS, 'St Martin' brougham coachwork by Brewster, an American coachbuilder closely associated with Rolls-Royce.

This superb drophead coupé was built by James Young Ltd on 1936 Phantom III chassis 3AX193.

Park Ward adapted its Bentley R-type Continental designs for the S1 Continental with only the most minor of changes other than lengthening to suit the 123-inch wheelbase of the S1 chassis. Both the two-door saloon and drophead coupé seen here were exceedingly handsome cars.

The H. J. Mulliner two-door Bentley Continental lost its former familiar 'fastback' outline to become arguably an even more strikingly handsome sports saloon. Note the then fashionable wrap-around windscreen and rear window.

When Rolls-Royce Ltd Car Division Managing Director Dr F. Llewellyn Smith and Chief Styling Engineer John Blatchley visited the Turin Motor Show in the late 1950s they admired an Alfa Romeo coupé designed by Swedish freelance stylist V. Koren. Thus inspired, the Company prevailed upon Mr Koren to work with Blatchley at Crewe to design the coachwork for the Bentley S2 Continental. The result was this sleek drophead coupé.

This is the author's 1966 Bentley T Series (chassis SBH1563), showing the early style of interior with deep, fully instrumented fascia and picnic tables behind the front seats. Both features were casualties of American-inspired 'Federal Safety Standard' (1968 for US exports, 1969 standard all markets).

Above: *The 1996 model year cars were announced at the Rolls-Royce Enthusiasts' Club Annual Rally at Althorp Park, Northamptonshire, in June 1995. The numerical appellation was dropped so that the Silver Spirit III and Silver Spur III were replaced by the Silver Spirit and Silver Spur, reverting to the original 1980 model names. This photograph of a 1996 model year Silver Spirit shows the higher-mounted, integrated bumpers and the absence of quarter-lights in the front doors to make way for the new external mirrors.*

Below: *The 1996 model year Silver Spur, showing the lower radiator shell and smaller Spirit of Ecstasy. Again, note the new external mirrors, which, along with the new adjustable steering wheel, are integrated into the seat memory positions so that one's favourite driving position is assumed at the push of a button.*

The 1996 MY Bentley Brooklands (above) and Turbo R (below), showing the lower grille, integrated bumpers, new external mirrors and revised wheels. The Brooklands has 16-inch wheels, the Turbo R 17-inch.

The new four-door saloon fascia features a centre console for both Rolls-Royce (left) and Bentley models. The Bentley centre console is shaped slightly differently to accommodate the gear selector, which is still on the steering column on the Rolls-Royce models. The Rolls-Royce fascia has more elaborate woodwork, with a crossbanded and boxwood-inlaid surround, while the Bentley has more comprehensive instrumentation, with rev counter. The CD player is normally concealed behind a veneered flap, shown open on the Rolls-Royce. The adjustable steering wheel is shown in its fully raised position on the Rolls-Royce.

The 1996 MY Bentley Continental R shares the 17-inch wheels of the Azure, a design that is a spin-off from the Concept Java project. Along with the other turbocharged Bentley models, the Continental R now provides 8 per cent more performance with 7 per cent better fuel economy. Despite weighing in at 2.4 tonnes, this ultimate supercar is capable of accelerating smoothly from standstill to 60 mph in under 6 seconds.

Displaying a similar wingline to the Bentley Mk VIs on page 64, this is Park Ward's Silver Wraith six-light saloon. This was an extremely popular design and was built from 1949 until the end of the short wheelbase chassis. The large boot and extensive window area made it particularly effective for touring. The headlamps were the built-in Silver Dawn type rather than the R.100 type that were almost universal on Silver Wraiths until that time. The photograph shows chassis WOF11, the 1951 Earls Court exhibit.

Among the best looking of the various coachbuilders' early post-war designs was H. J. Mulliner's 'Lightweight' saloon on the Bentley Mk VI (and later R-type) chassis. Not only was the shape entirely new, but so was the method of construction, using extruded light alloy framing with aluminium panels. The masterful styling has more in common with the later S Series cars than with the Mk VI standard saloon. For the premium price of £5,105 (the standard steel saloon cost £3,674 in late 1950) one had a more imposing and modern-looking motor car with a much larger boot.

From June 1952 numerous changes were introduced with the 'R' series Bentley and the 'E' series Silver Dawn chassis to correspond with new standard steel coachwork with longer boot; this is a Silver Dawn chassis. The automatic gearbox was available only on export cars at first, but later also on home market cars. Early chassis frames were riveted, but commencing with chassis B349TO (Bentley) and SNF1 (Silver Dawn) the frame was of welded construction as seen here. The dual exhaust system was standard on the Bentley R-type and first appeared on the Silver Dawn from the start of the 'H' series.

Later in 1952 (June) a magnificent new version of the Bentley Mk VI was introduced. This was the Bentley Continental, which rejoiced in higher gearing, a special low-loss exhaust system and lightweight, streamlined, two-door coachwork by H. J. Mulliner. This model later became known as the Bentley R-type Continental to distinguish it from the subsequent S-type Continental, though the first few cars were based on the Mk VI chassis and their specification meant that strictly speaking they should be classified as Mk VI Continentals. At first the Continental was an export-only model, though it later became available on the home market where it was eagerly sought by wealthy performance-minded motorists who wanted the absolute ultimate in high-speed luxury transport. The ability to run up to 100 mph in third gear and a top speed just short of 120 mph meant that this was the fastest genuine four-seater car in the world at the time, which says a great deal for the early post-war chassis design.

In July 1952 the standard steel saloon coachwork for the Silver Dawn and Bentley models was modified with a much-needed larger boot and modified rear wings, with changes to the rear suspension to cope with the longer overhang. These changes occurred at the 'E' series Silver Dawn and 'R' series Bentley, the latter of which later became known as the R-type.

Another 1952 development was the introduction of an automatic gearbox.

A shortcoming of the Bentley Mk VI and early Silver Dawn standard steel saloons was a serious deficiency of luggage space. The task of addressing this problem fell to then chief styling engineer John Blatchley, who redesigned the tail of the car for the Bentley VII and 'E' series Silver Dawn. This is an experimental Bentley VII, or R-type, chassis 12BVII. The extended rear wing and longer boot made for a sleeker-looking car than its short-boot predecessor, particularly when viewed from the three-quarter rear aspect.

Unlike that of the short-boot car, the boot lid was hinged at the top and a great deal more luggage could be accommodated. The self-supporting boot lid was of aluminium alloy. Note the large spanner for the wheel disc nuts.

The Company had studied the automatic and semi-automatic transmission systems then available and, rejecting the ponderous 'preselector' gearboxes used by some British manufacturers at the time, opted instead for the excellent General Motors 'Hydra-Matic' automatic gearbox and fluid coupling. At first these were bought-out straight from GM's Detroit Transmission Division, and, due to foreign exchange restrictions still in force at that time, cars so fitted were available for export only. By early in 1953 a special department at Crewe had been set up to manufacture the gearbox under licence and it became available for home market orders. Being a four-speed unit it was superior to most other automatic gearboxes of the period and the chosen ratios closely approximated those of the synchromesh gearbox. A beautifully made selector mounted on the steering column allowed both second and third gears to be held by the driver for maximum acceleration or engine braking, with an automatic up-change to top gear in position '3' to prevent over-revving of the engine. The automatic gearbox was available on all Rolls-Royce and Bentley models.

At first there was no Phantom model in the post-war range of cars as

The long-boot standard steel saloon in Silver Dawn (left) and the Bentley R-type guises. The design lent itself particularly well to two-tone paint schemes.

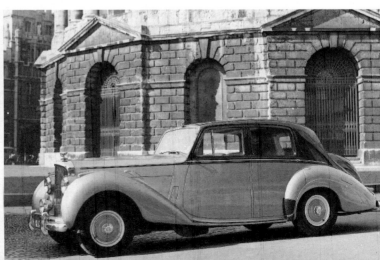

James Young built a small series of saloon bodies on late Silver Dawn chassis.

Hooper's Chief Designer, Osmond Rivers, was the creator of this bold and innovative styling on the Bentley Mk VI and R-type (seen here), Silver Dawn and Silver Wraith chassis. The front wings flowed gently down in a concave line to the base of the tail. The absence of separate rear wings enabled the interior, particularly the rear compartment, to have greater effective width.

Later Park Ward drophead coupes were fully coachbuilt and no longer used the standard steel saloon front wings. This very satisfactory design is shown with the power-operated hood in the raised position. It was offered on the Silver Dawn chassis (shown) as well as on the late Bentley Mk VI, R-type and, in a larger version, the Silver Wraith chassis.

Special coachwork on the Silver Dawn chassis is in any case unusual, but this saloon, photographed by Thomas T. Solley (RREC) while in his ownership, is particularly so. It is chassis LSTH22, bodied by the Italian coachbuilder Ghia and exhibited by that firm at the 1952 Turin Motor Show. The radiator shell was reduced in height by the coachbuilder and mounted forward of its normal position in order to blend with the lines of the coachwork. Note the front bumper with its special mounting for the small Italian number plate.

In late 1950 H. J. Mulliner's Silver Wraith touring limousine was transformed into an exceedingly handsome six-light form with a higher front wingline, top-hinged boot lid and push-button door handles. When the original short wheelbase chassis was discontinued this design was extended for the long wheelbase chassis. The result was this exceptionally smart-looking motor car.

For the long wheelbase Silver Wraith chassis Park Ward offered this fine touring saloon. The reversion to the original (standing) Spirit of Ecstasy and the Silver Cloud-style built-in headlights and bumper overriders indicate an 'E' series (late 1955) or later car.

The long wheelbase Silver Wraith chassis was particularly well suited to seven-seater limousine coachwork. This rounded style was the work of Park Ward & Co.

Park Ward built eight handsome drophead coupés of ample proportions on the Silver Wraith long wheelbase chassis. This is chassis DLW149.

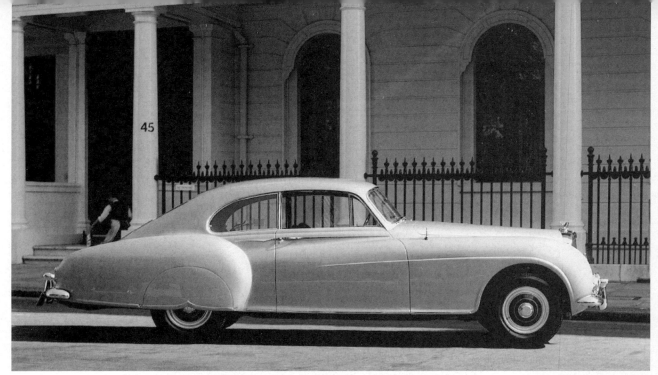

The Bentley R-type Continental, introduced in 1952. The sleek H. J. Mulliner coachwork was wind-tunnel proven and built with weight minimisation in mind. It was the fastest genuine four-seater car in the world at the time, being capable of 100 mph in third gear!

The Phantom IV, at 12 ft 1 in wheelbase, was the longest of the early post-war chassis. This is 4AF2, the first Phantom IV, built to the order of the then Princess Elizabeth and the Duke of Edinburgh. H. J. Mulliner & Co were entrusted with the design and construction of the coachwork of this car, as indeed they were for just over half of the Phantom IVs. A youthful Queen Elizabeth II is seen in the rear compartment before an enthusiastic crowd. Note that the royal car is fitted with a blue police light or 'theatre light' above the windscreen and fittings for the attachment of the Royal Standard on the front of the roof. A special mascot depicting St George slaying the dragon replaces the Spirit of Ecstasy.

Three Phantom IVs – two limousines and a cabriolet – were built with elaborate armour plating for General Franco of Spain; H. J. Mulliner & Co designed and built the coachwork. This photograph of the cabriolet, chassis 4AF18, shows the hood in the raised position.

Chassis 4AF20 is a very elegant Hooper sedanca de ville, the only body of that type on a Phantom IV chassis. The paintwork was dark green with a lighter green band at the waistline, while the interior upholstery was in red Connolly hide. It was shipped to France on 6 April 1952 for delivery to its owner, HH Prince Aga Khan.

Hooper's styling features seen and described elsewhere translated particularly elegantly to a chassis of the Phantom IV's length. This is chassis 4BP3, a Hooper limousine built for HRH The Prince Regent of Iraq.

it was felt that the social and economic climates were not compatible with such extravagance. However, as mentioned above, there was an eight-cylinder engine available in the Rationalised Range and the chassis design allowed for larger (Phantom) models. Therefore, when an order was received from HRH Princess Elizabeth (later HM Queen Elizabeth II) and the Duke of Edinburgh for a much larger car than the Silver Wraith, and apparently specifying the eight-cylinder engine of which the Duke had knowledge through his experiences with the experimental 'Scalded Cat' Bentley, the Company was perfectly able and willing to oblige. In view of the Company's desire to take over the historic role of Daimler in supplying motor cars to the reigning monarch, eager to oblige might be more accurate!

Thus the first Phantom IV was delivered in 1950. Not wishing to make this model available for general consumption, the Company accepted subsequent orders only from royalty and heads of state. Only 18 were built, one being retained by the Company as a test vehicle. The Phantom IV was thus the most exclusive Rolls-Royce ever and the only one to be powered by a straight-eight engine.

TECHNICAL SPECIFICATIONS

Silver Wraith, Silver Dawn, Bentley Mk VI and R-type, 1946-1959.

Engine

Six cylinders in line. Iron monobloc casting, top 2¼ inches of bores 'flash-chromed'. Aluminium alloy cylinder head.
Bore 3.5 inches (89 mm), stroke 4.5 inches (114 mm), cubic capacity 4,257 cc. Overhead inlet and side exhaust valves, single gear-driven camshaft. Seven-bearing crankshaft. Twin SU carburetters (right-hand-drive Bentley Mk VI and all R-type) or Stromberg dual-choke carburetter (Silver Wraith, Silver Dawn and left-hand-drive Bentley Mk VI).

1948: Short 30% chrome iron liners in tops of bores.
1952 (Silver Wraith and Silver Dawn): Zenith single-choke carburetter.
1954 (Bentley Continental), 1955 (Silver Wraith long wheelbase): Bore 3.75 inches (95.25 mm), stroke 4.5 inches (114 mm), cubic capacity 4,887 cc with full-length pressed-in liners.

1956 (Silver Wraith long wheelbase): Twin SU carburetters.

Chassis

Channel-section frame of riveted construction with cruciform centre-bracing.

1953: Welded construction.

Overall length 17 ft 2 in (5,232 mm) (Silver Wraith short wheelbase), 17 ft 9½ in (5,423 mm) (Silver Wraith long wheelbase), 16 ft 0 in (4,877 mm) (Silver Dawn as introduced and Bentley Mk VI). *These are minimum dimensions; the overall length varied according to the design of coachwork and types of export and later bumpers, which added to these dimensions.*
Wheelbase 10 ft 7 in (3,226 mm) (Silver Wraith short wheelbase), 11 ft 1 in (3,378 mm) (Silver Wraith long wheelbase), 10 ft 0 in (3,048 mm) (Silver Dawn and Bentley).

Transmission

Four forward speeds and reverse. Right-hand change (column change on left-hand-drive cars). Synchromesh on second, third and top gears. Gearbox ratios: top 1:1, third 1.343:1, second 2.02:1, first

2.985:1, reverse 3.15:1.
Single dry-plate, centrifugally assisted clutch.

1952 (optional): Rolls-Royce four-speed automatic gearbox and fluid coupling, with selector mounted on the right of the steering column. Ratios: top 1:1, third 1.45:1, second 2.63:1, first 3.82:1, reverse 3.15:1.

Two-piece propeller shaft with needle roller bearing universal joints and centre bearing.
Semi-floating type with hypoid gears. Ratio: 3.727:1.

1951 (Silver Wraith long wheelbase): 3.416:1 optional.
1952 (Bentley Continental): 3.077:1.
1953 (optional on Bentley R-type): 3.416:1.
1954 (Bentley R-type and Silver Dawn): 3.416:1.
1955 (Silver Wraith long wheelbase): 4.25:1.
1956 (Silver Wraith long wheelbase): 4.375:1 (3.416:1 for certain export markets).

Steering

Marles-type cam and roller. Fore and aft side steering tube (drag link) to centre steering lever pivoted on front chassis cross-member and two-piece cross steering tube (track rod). Turns lock to lock, 3½.
Power-assisted steering offered as option from the Silver Wraith long wheelbase 'F' series onwards.

Suspension

Front: independent by coil springs and rubber-bushed wishbones, double-acting hydraulic dampers and anti-roll bar.
Rear: semi-elliptic leaf springs protected by leather gaiters. Controllable hydraulic dampers by oil pump mounted on gearbox and overriding control on steering wheel boss.
Silver Wraith long wheelbase with power-assisted steering had electrically operated controllable dampers operated from switch on side of steering column.

Brakes

Hydraulic front, mechanical rear. Operation by means of friction disc servo on offside of gearbox, which applies front brakes through a Lockheed master cylinder and assists application of rear brakes. Handbrake on rear wheels by pull-out handle under right side of facia through cable and mechanical linkage.

Chassis lubrication system

All bearings in steering and suspension systems, including rear spring main leaf and shackles, fed with oil from reservoir and pump mounted on bulkhead in engine compartment. Pump operated by pedal under facia, to be operated once every 100 miles (160 km).

Fuel system

Rear-mounted petrol tank, capacity 18 gallons (21.6 US gallons, 81.8 litres). SU dual fuel pump mounted in frame. Filter between tank and pump.

Road wheels and tyres

Silver Dawn and Bentley: 16-inch steel disc well-base wheels, on five studs, carrying 6.50 x 16 India tyres.
Silver Wraith: 17-inch steel disc well-base wheels, on five studs, carrying 6.50 x 17 Dunlop Fort tyres.

1951 (Silver Wraith long and short wheelbase cars for certain markets): 16-inch wheels with 7.50 x 16 tyres.

CHASSIS NUMBERS

Silver Wraith chassis were numbered consecutively, omitting 13.

Silver Wraith short wheelbase

Chassis numbers	Year
WTA1-85, WVA1-81, WYA1-87	1946-48
WZB1-65, WAB1-65, WCB1-73	1948-49
WDC1-101, WFC1-101, WGC1-101	1948-50
WHD1-101	1950
WLE1-35, WME1-96	1950-51
WOF1-76	1951-52
WSG1-76	1952
WVH1-116	1952-53

Total: 1,244 cars.

Silver Wraith long wheelbase

Chassis numbers	Year
ALW1-51	1952-53
BLW1-101	1953-54
CLW1-43	1954
DLW1-172	1954-55
ELW1-101	1955-56
FLW1-101	1956-57
GLW1-26	1957-58
HLW1-52	1958

Total: 639 cars.

Total Silver Wraiths built: 1,883 cars.

Bentley Mk VI

Chassis series and sub-series starting with 1 use odd numbers only, omitting 13. Those starting with 2 use even numbers only.

Chassis numbers	Year
B2AK-B254AK*, B1AJ-B247AJ	1946-47
B2BH-B400BH, B1BG-B401BG	1947-48
B2CF-B500CF, B1CD-B501CD	1947-48
B2DA-B500DA, B1DZ-B501DZ	1948-49
B2EY-B500EY, B1EW-B501EW	1949-50
B2FV-B500FV, B1FU-B601FU	1949-50
B1GT-B401GT	1950
B2HR-B250HR, B1HP-B251HP	1950-51
B2JO-B250JO, B1JN-B251JN	1950-51
B2KM-B200KM, B1KL-B201KL	1951
B2LJ-B400LJ, B1LH-B401LH	1951
B2MD-B400MD, B1MB-B401MB*	1951-52
B2NZ-B500NZ, B1NY-B501NY	1951-52

B2PV-B300PV, B1PU-B301PU 1952

* Plus experimental cars 1BVI and 4BVI, later renumbered B256AK and B403MB respectively.

Total: 5,202 cars.

Bentley R-type

Chassis series and sub-series starting with 1 use odd numbers only, omitting 13. Those starting with 2 use even numbers only.

Chassis numbers	Year
B2RT-B120RT*, B1RS-B121RS	1952-53
B2SR-B500SR, B1SP-B501SP	1952-53
B1TO-B401TO, B2TN-B600TN	1953
B1UL-B251UL, B2UM-B250UM	1953-54
B2WH-B300WH, B1WG-B301WG	1954
B2XF-B140XF	1954
B1YA-B331YA, B2YD-B330YD	1954
B1ZX-B251ZX, B2ZY-B250ZY	1954-55

* Plus experimental cars 12BVII and 14BVII, later renumbered B124XRT and B122XRT respectively.

Total: 2,322 cars.

Bentley R-type Continental

Chassis are numbered consecutively, omitting 13.

Chassis numbers	Year
BC1A-BC25A*	1952-1953
BC1B-BC25B	1953
BC1C-BC78C	1953-1954
BC1D-BC74D	1954-1955
BC1E-BC9E	1955

* Plus experimental car 9BVI, later renumbered BC26A.

Total: 208 cars.

Silver Dawn

Chassis series and sub-series starting with 1 use odd numbers only, omitting 13. Those starting with 2 use even numbers only.

Chassis numbers	Year
SBA2-138, SCA1-63	1949-1951
SDB2-140	1950-51
SFC2-160	1951-52
SHD2-60	1952
SKE2-50, SLE1-51	1952-53
SMF2-76, SNF1-125	1952-54
SOG2-100, SPG1-101	1954
SRH2-100, STH1-101	1954
SUJ2-130, SVJ1-133	1954-55

Total: 761 cars.

PHANTOM IV

As Silver Wraith, except:

Engine

Eight cylinders in line.
A & B series: Bore 3.5 inches (89 mm), stroke 4.5 inches (114 mm), cubic capacity 5,675 cc.
C series: Bore 3.75 inches (95.25 mm), stroke 4.5 inches (114 mm), cubic capacity 6,515 cc.
Nine-bearing crankshaft.

Chassis

Overall length 19 ft 1.5 in (5,829 mm)
Wheelbase 12 ft 1 in (3,683 mm)

Transmission

Automatic gearbox introduced for 'B' series.
Rear axle ratio: 4.25:1.

Fuel system

Petrol filler necks on both sides of car, capacity 23 gallons (27.6 US gallons, 104.5 litres).

Road wheels and tyres

17-inch steel disc wheels with semi-drop centre rims, on ten studs, carrying 7.00 x 17 Dunlop Fort 'C' tyres.
B & C series cars: 8.00 x 17 tyres.

CHASSIS NUMBERS

Chassis series starting with 1 use odd numbers only, omitting 13. Those starting with 2 use even numbers only.

Chassis numbers	Year
4AF1-4AF22	1950-52
4BP1-4BP7	1953-55
4CS2-4CS6	1955-56

Total: 18 cars.

Chapter Six

The Silver Cloud

By 1952 the Silver Dawn and Bentley R-type Standard Saloons were looking decidedly dated. Their chassis was basically pre-war in concept and the lengthening of the body to provide a longer boot did little to disguise the otherwise 1946 styling. The end for these models came in the spring of 1955, the last deliveries being made in May of that year. Deliveries of the all-new Silver Cloud and Bentley S-type had commenced the previous month.

To the casual observer the sleek new standard saloon coachwork with utterly flawless lines was the main change from the previous models. However, the exterior hid a whole host of technical improvements. The chassis was all new and the six-cylinder engine was bigger and more powerful. For the first time Rolls-Royce and Bentley models shared exactly the same engine, the twin SU carburetters formerly used only for the Bentleys being standardised for both versions.

The Silver Cloud chassis frame was of welded box-section and was much stronger and stiffer than that of its predecessors. The semi-trailing independent front suspension was also new, while the semi-elliptic rear springs were mounted inboard of the chassis rails and a 'Z'-type axle control rod was fitted on the off-side to check roll and control spring wind-up. The rear shock dampers were still controllable, but this was now achieved by means of a solenoid in the dampers controlled by a switch on the side of the steering column, thus eliminating the last control from the steering wheel boss. These features, together with smaller (15-inch) wheels carrying wider (8.20-inch) tyres with wider front and rear track combined to give the new cars

Unlike its predecessors, the Silver Cloud and Bentley S Series chassis frame was of welded box-section. The 'Z'-type axle control rod can be seen between the off-side main frame member and the rear axle. The Bentley S Series chassis was identical except for radiator shell and badging.

A lovely publicity shot of a Silver Cloud which as well as showing to full advantage the flawless lines of the standard saloon coachwork – the work of John Blatchley and his Crewe design team – also shows how very well suited the design was to two-tone paint. The Silver Cloud was equally at home in London or New York, Los Angeles or Melbourne – or in English countryside. The remaining specialist coachbuilders were hard pressed to better either the beautiful external lines or the extremely high standard of interior furnishings. These superb cars seldom fail to impress, even into in their fifth decade.

This view shows the alternative Bentley S-type, for which more customers opted than the statelier Rolls-Royce version. On the Bentley S-type, the 'winged-B' mascot was not mounted on a dummy filler cap as it had been on the earlier models.

An evocative photograph of an early Silver Cloud alongside a contemporary Rolls-Royce 'Avon'-powered Comet 4 jet airliner.

superior handling characteristics and smoother ride.

The braking system, while still based on the traditional friction-disc servo, was the subject of considerable improvement. The front brakes were of the two-trailing-shoe type, to avoid the 'self-servo' action of leading shoes relied upon by certain other makers to provide a light pedal but notorious for causing fade under severe conditions of use. At the rear, leading and trailing shoes were used. For the first time, both front and rear brakes were hydraulically actuated, though the direct mechanical linkage between the pedal and the rear brakes was retained, mainly to impart 'feel' to the pedal. There was an increase in friction area amounting to almost 30 per cent despite the reduced drum diameter. This new braking system provided smooth, powerful, fade-free braking from the high speeds of which the car was so effortlessly capable, with pedal pressures so light that road-testers invariably expressed amazement.

From May 1956 the master cylinder and fluid reservoir were duplicated,

A severe test of good styling is how it looks from the rear. This three-quarter rear shot of a Silver Cloud shows how convincingly John Blatchley's standard saloon design passes this test.

with an extra set of expanders for the front shoes. The system was split so that one circuit activated one shoe in each front drum while the other worked the rear brakes and the remaining shoes at the front. Thus, with the pedal still mechanically linked to the rear brakes, the system was effectively triplicated and thus virtually immune to failure.

By increasing the bore by ⅛ inch to 3¾ inches, the 'F'-head six-cylinder engine was raised in swept volume to 4,887 cc. The cylinder head was entirely redesigned with six ports for better breathing and increased power. The 'flash-chroming' of the tops of the bores of the early post-war engines had not been a conspicuous success and short pressed-in liners were later substituted. For the Silver Cloud and S Series, however, full-length liners were pressed into the block to provide a continuous wear resistant surface all the way down the bores. The pistons were fitted with four rings – the top one chromium-plated. Twin SU type HD.6 carburetters were fitted to both Rolls-Royce and Bentley versions.

For all the mechanical improvements, which endowed the Silver Cloud and Bentley S Series cars with performance to match the sleek new looks, it was undoubtedly the latter attribute that attracted the most attention and the new models were an instant hit in the United States, particularly the Rolls-Royce version as the Bentley marque was still relatively unknown there.

The standard saloons were particularly appealing for their superb lines and interior luxury. They were so good, in fact, that the coachbuilders were hard pressed to better them. The steel body shell was extremely rigid and strong while weight was minimised by the use of aluminium for the doors, bonnet and boot. The windscreen was of curved 'Triplex' glass and the rear window, which was also curved, was much larger than that of previous standard saloons. Like some previous coachbuilt cars, the doors of the new cars were of the 'half-frame' variety, ie with slim bright metal frames to the tops of the doors around the windows. These were stainless steel rather than chromium-plated brass as used by the coachbuilders. The effect was a light and airy appearance with maximum glass area and minimum weight.

The standard saloon's interior was the very model of sumptuous luxury. It was uncommonly spacious, with ample legroom in both front and rear compartments, while the seating was extremely comfortable and well designed. The front seat was a bench-type with separate squabs, each of which could be reclined individually, and three people could be carried thereon if necessary. The rear seat squab was shaped for maximum comfort for two passengers, with an ample centre armrest, but three could be accommodated with ease.

The only features missing, as *The Autocar* pointed out in its 1955 road test, were folding centre armrests in

No less handsome was the standard saloon's interior, which set new standards of luxury. The tasteful fascia in particular lent the front compartment an air of unostentatious luxury. The switch on the left of the steering column is for the electrically adjustable rear shock dampers.

Top: *All the luxury features of the earlier standard saloons were retained and improved for the Silver Cloud and S-type interior. The rear seat in particular was even more luxurious than hitherto, with more legroom, generous corner padding and ample support for shoulders and thighs.*

Left: *The front seat was a bench type with separate reclining squabs. The centre armrests shown were absent in the earliest cars. The side armrests are adjustable both fore and aft, and for height.*

the front seat; to show that the Company takes notice these were duly added early in 1956.

Customers could still choose a coachbuilt car in order to have something different and more individual, but it is arguable whether the coachbuilt bodies actually improved on the standard saloon's looks or interior appointments, and some clearly did not. In fact most of the coachbuilders' offerings continued to be concentrated on the Silver Wraith

chassis, which remained in production to cater for the carriage trade, and on that of the Bentley Continental.

The Continental variant of the Bentley S-type differed from the standard chassis mainly in its higher gearing and lower radiator. The synchromesh gearbox was still available on this chassis at first, but few buyers took up this option and it was soon withdrawn. All Rolls-Royce and Bentley cars have been automatic ever since.

The coachwork for the Bentley Continental was provided by outside coachbuilders – mainly H. J. Mulliner and Park Ward. A few bodies were built by James Young and even fewer by Hooper.

Towards the end of 1957 a long wheelbase version of the standard chassis became available, 4 inches longer but otherwise similar in its engine and chassis details. A longer version of the standard saloon coachwork was offered on this

For the Silver Cloud and Bentley S-type, Harold Radford (Coachbuilders) Ltd offered a 'Countryman' conversion of the standard saloon that included every conceivable luxury fitting. Each feature was available, and priced, separately so that the customer could choose a uniquely individual package. Thus each 'Countryman' is different and unique. The photograph shows the 'Webasto' sunshine roof, which was one of the more popular Radford modifications. The ample front doors allowed the fitting of compartments for glasses, decanters and flasks therein. John Bull's drawing depicts the picnic requisites, including electric kettle and washbasin, that were among the fittings available for the boot.

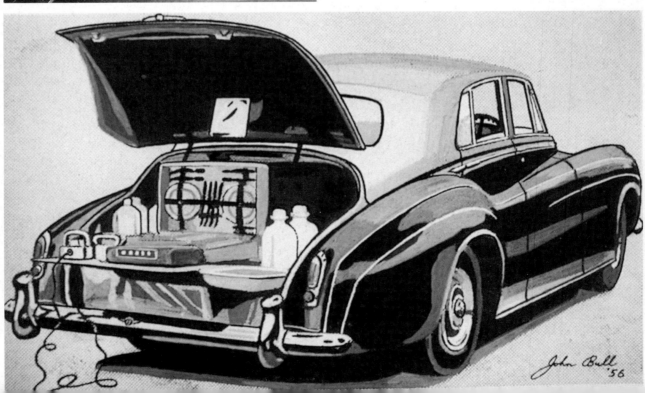

H. J. Mulliner's work on the Silver Cloud and Bentley S Series chassis comprised saloon and drophead coupé designs sharing a common wingline and boot shape. The first photograph (above) shows a six-light saloon on a Bentley chassis. This was a natural development of Mulliner's 'Lightweight' saloons on the Mk VI and R-type chassis, using the same mode of construction. Note the rear-hinged doors to the rear compartment – a rare feature on all but formal limousines by the mid-'fifties. The similarly styled drophead coupé (below) was offered by H. J. Mulliner until mid-1959, when the firm changed over to adapting standard saloons to dropheads.

JACK BARCLAY LTD.

James Young Ltd offered this smart alternative (seen in the first photograph – above) to the standard saloon on the Silver Cloud and Bentley S chassis. The example shown is Silver Cloud I chassis SWA52, the company's 1955 Earls Court Show exhibit. There was also a superb and very rare drophead coupé. The first of these, on 1958 chassis LSGE448, is seen in the second view in the coachbuilder's official photograph.

Hoopers developed this distinctive styling for the Silver Cloud and S Series. Note the rear-hinged doors to the rear compartment and the hooded headlamps mounted on the extremities of the front wings.

Freestone & Webb built fewer bodies than the other main coachbuilders, and produced more 'one-off' designs, of which this six-light saloon on Silver Cloud I chassis SYB24 is one. Note the heavily hooded headlights and rear lights, and the straight-through wingline.

chassis, usually with a division. The body shells for this type of coachwork were produced by Park Ward in Willesden by cutting and extending standard saloon bodies. Once modified, these body shells were transported to Crewe where they were mounted on their chassis, painted, trimmed and finished.

One of the first major changes to occur to the Silver Cloud and Bentley S Series was the option of power-assisted steering (what we would call today simply power steering). Because of the lead time between the ordering of a coachbuilt car and its completion and delivery, the Company found itself in the position of having to fit this

option, at no little expense, to some chassis already delivered to the coachbuilders, in response to customer demands that their car should be of the latest specification.

The later cars also had a higher compression ratio, larger (type HD.8) carburetters, larger inlet valves and stronger rear axle half-shafts.

In early 1959 H. J. Mulliner began modifying and adapting standard saloon bodies to this drophead coupé form. This proved so commercially successful that from that time the company's efforts on standard Silver Cloud and Bentley S Series chassis were confined to this style. The body shells, once converted, were returned to Crewe for mounting on the chassis, followed by wiring, painting and interior trimming. The car was then returned to Mulliner's for installation of the hood and its mechanism. With the fully lined hood raised, the car was as comfortable and draught-free as a saloon.

TECHNICAL SPECIFICATIONS

Silver Cloud and Bentley S Type

Engine

Six cylinders in line. Iron monobloc casting with full-length high chrome content liners. Aluminium alloy cylinder head.
Bore 3.75 inches (95.25 mm), stroke 4.5 inches (114 mm), cubic capacity 4,887 cc. Overhead inlet and side exhaust valves, single gear-driven camshaft. Seven-bearing crankshaft. Twin SU carburetters with automatic choke.

Chassis

Welded box-section frame with cruciform centre-bracing.
Overall length 17 ft 8 in (5,385 mm) (standard and Continental), 17 ft 11¾ in (5,480 mm) (long wheelbase). Wheelbase 10 ft 3 in (3,124 mm) (standard and Continental), 10 ft 7 in (3,226 mm) (long wheelbase).

Transmission

Rolls-Royce four-speed automatic gearbox and fluid coupling, with selector mounted on right of steering column. Ratios: top 1:1, third 1.45:1, second 2.63:1, first 3.82:1, reverse 4.3:1.
Manual gearbox, with right-hand change lever, available on early Bentley Continental S-type.
Two-piece propeller shaft with needle roller bearing universal joints and centre bearing.
Rear axle: hypoid bevel final drive with four-star differential and semi-floating half-shafts. Ratio 3.42:1 (2.92:1 on Bentley Continental).

Steering

Marles-type cam and roller connected by transverse link to three-piece track linkage. Power-assisted steering optional, at first for export only, from Silver Cloud mid-'C' series, Bentley late-'B' series, Bentley Continental early 'B' series and all long wheelbase cars. Turns, lock to lock, 4¼.

Suspension

Front: independent by coil springs, opposed piston hydraulic dampers and anti-roll bar.
Rear: semi-elliptic leaf springs protected by leather gaiters. Electrically controllable hydraulic dampers by switch on left of steering column to give 'normal' or 'hard' setting.

Brakes

Rolls-Royce/Girling drum brakes. Hydraulic front, hydraulic/mechanical rear. Operation by means of friction disc servo on offside of gearbox, which applies brakes hydraulically. Handbrake on rear wheels by pull-out, twist-to-release handle under facia through cable and mechanical linkage.

1956 (including long wheelbase cars from introduction): Twin master cylinders and duplicated front hydraulic circuits.

Chassis lubrication system

Limited centralised system supplying bearings in steering and front suspension, with oil from reservoir and pump mounted on bulkhead in engine compartment. Pump operated by pedal under facia, to be operated once every 100 miles (160 km). Rear springs packed with grease for life.

Fuel system

Rear-mounted petrol tank, capacity 18 gallons (21.6 US gallons, 81.8 litres). SU dual fuel pump mounted in frame. Filter between tank and pump.

Road wheels and tyres

15-inch steel disc wheels, on five studs, carrying 8.20 x 15 broad base tyres. Bentley Continentals had either 7.60 x 15 or 8.00 x 15 tyres depending on body type.

CHASSIS AND ENGINE NUMBERS

Silver Cloud I

Chassis sub-series starting with 1 use odd numbers only, omitting 13. Those starting with 2 use even numbers only.

Chassis numbers	Year
SWA2-250, SXA1-252	1955-56
SYB2-250, SZB1-251	1956
SBC2-150, SCC1-151	1956-57
SDD2-450, SED1-451	1957-58
SGE2-500, SFE1-501	1957-59
SHF1-249, SJF2-250	1958-59
SKG1-125, SLG2-126	1959
SMH1-265, SNH2-262	1959

Total: 2,238 cars.

Bentley S1

Chassis sub-series starting with 1 use odd numbers only, omitting 13. Those starting with 2 use even numbers only.

Chassis numbers	Year
B2AN-B500AN, B1AP-B501AP	1955-56
B2BA-B250BA, B1BC-B251BC	1956
B2CK-B500CK, B1CM-B500CM	1956
B2DB-B350DB, B1DE-B351DE	1956-57
B2EG-B650EG, B1EK-B651EK	1957
B2FA-B650FA, B1FD-B651FD	1957-59
B1GD-B125GD, B2GC-B126GC	1959
B1HB-B45HB, B2HA-B50HA	1959

Total: 3,072 cars.

Silver Cloud I long wheelbase

Chassis are numbered consecutively, omitting 13.

Chassis numbers	Year
ALC1-26*	1957-58
BLC1-51	1958-59
CLC1-47	1958-59

* Plus experimental car 28B, later renumbered ALC1X.

Total: 122 cars.

Bentley S1 long wheelbase

Chassis are numbered consecutively, omitting 13.

Chassis numbers	Year
ALB1-36	1957-59

Total: 35 cars.

Bentley Continental S1

Chassis are numbered consecutively, omitting 13.

Chassis numbers	Year
BC1AF-BC102AF	1955-56
BC1BG-BC101BG	1956-57
BC1CH-BC51CH	1957
BC1DJ-BC51DJ	1957-58
BC1EL-BC51EL	1957-58
BC1FM-BC51FM	1958-59
BC1GN-BC31GN	1958-59

Total: 431 cars.

Chapter Seven

Faster Clouds and the Phantom V

With the introduction of the 6¼-litre aluminium alloy V-8 engine in the autumn of 1959, the Rolls-Royce Silver Cloud and Bentley S-type became the Silver Cloud II and Bentley S2 respectively. At the same time, the Silver Wraith was discontinued and a Phantom model was made generally available for the first time since 1939. This was the Phantom V, of which more anon.

Though the V-8 engine was considerably wider as well as, of course, shorter than the six-cylinder, and was obviously designed with future models in mind, it was able to be fitted into the Silver Cloud. To make room for it the steering box had to be moved from the inside to the outside of the chassis frame, and a pair of pinions was provided to retain the lateral position of the steering column, which was shorter and more steeply raked. As power-assisted steering was now standard, the steering wheel was smaller and its rim slimmer; because the column was shorter the wheel was closer to the fascia, providing a more comfortable driving position.

The standard saloon coachwork remained unchanged for the Silver Cloud II and Bentley S2 except for some minor changes to the layout of the fascia, which now had a 120 mph speedometer to reflect the higher performance available from the V-8 engine.

The 6,230 cc V-8 engine – painted in grey for photographic purposes – as fitted to the Silver Cloud II, Bentley S2 and AS to CG series Phantom V. The carburetters are 1¾-inch SU type HD.6, similar to those of the early six-cylinder Silver Cloud/S Series engine. The engine is fitted with the pump and reservoir for the standard power-assisted steering, and on the far side the compressor for the optional refrigerated air conditioning can be glimpsed.

Externally, the standard saloon coachwork did not change for the Silver Cloud II and Bentley S2 – and why should it have? Its beauty of line was immune to the dictates of fashion and spoke for itself. These two photographs show how well the design lent itself to two-tone colour schemes.

For the Silver Cloud II and Bentley S2 standard chassis, H. J. Mulliner continued to adapt the standard saloon body shells to produce this beautiful and highly desirable drophead coupé.

A Continental version of the Bentley S2 chassis was offered. This had a lower radiator, four-shoe front brakes and, at first, a higher rear axle ratio. A choice of sleek, sporting coachwork was offered by Park Ward, H. J. Mulliner and James Young. Hooper was closing its coachbuilding operations and only built one body on the Bentley Continental S2 chassis.

Like the earlier Silver Clouds and S Series cars, the Silver Cloud II and Bentley S2 were available in long wheelbase guise. The chassis was 4 inches longer than standard and was fitted with a suitably lengthened standard saloon body, usually with a division. The task of extending the bodies was entrusted to Park Ward in London, with the painting, interior trimming and finishing work being carried out at Crewe on the standard saloon build lines. There was also a particularly handsome but much more expensive coachbuilt version by James Young.

Because the Phantom IV had been limited to royalty and heads of state, the demand for a really stately limousine was largely met until 1958 by the Silver Wraith, which had remained in production in long wheelbase form alongside the Silver Cloud, sharing the same 4.9-litre engine from 1956. The remainder of the Silver Wraith chassis was, however, of basically 1946 design, as were some of the body styles mounted thereon. It was not quite

The H. J. Mulliner two-door Bentley Continental lost its former familiar 'fastback' outline to become arguably an even more strikingly handsome sports saloon. Note the then fashionable wrap-around windscreen and rear window.

H. J. Mulliner's 'Flying Spur' saloon was continued for the S2 Continental, with the bonnet lowered at the front to suit the squatter radiator shell.

long enough to carry limousine coachwork combining really huge rear compartments with long, capacious luggage boots. Really spacious seven-seater limousines on the Silver Wraith chassis all suffered from stunted luggage boots that not only limited the luggage carrying capacity of the car but all too often marred the otherwise graceful lines.

The introduction of the V-8 engine in 1959 allowed the Silver Wraith to be discontinued and replaced with the Phantom V, which with a wheelbase the same as that of the Phantom IV (145 inches), overall length within 2 inches of 20 feet and engine carried well forward over the front axle, was ideally suited to limousine coachwork. For the first time coachbuilders were able to provide the desirable combination of an extraordinarily spacious rear compartment with a long, gracefully shaped, commodious boot.

The Phantom V chassis was a much-lengthened version of the Silver Cloud II chassis, with an enormous

This photograph shows how James Young's four-door sports saloon coachwork for the S2 Continental had developed into a six-light design, though retaining unchanged the wingline of the six-cylinder car.

The long wheelbase adaptation of the standard saloon was continued for the Silver Cloud II range. The extending and modifying of the body shells was carried out by Park Ward at Willesden, the interiors and finishing by Rolls-Royce at Crewe.

The Silver Cloud II (and Bentley S2) long-wheelbase chassis was also made available for special coachwork. This is the saloon with division by James Young Ltd.

H. J. Mulliner built this superb cabriolet on Silver Cloud II long wheelbase chassis LLCB16. It is photographed outside the Park Ward offices in Willesden, which were at that time used by the combined firm H. J. Mulliner, Park Ward Ltd, but sadly were demolished in 1982.

This is Park Ward's standard seven-passenger limousine design for the Phantom V up to and including the CG series. Styling was the work of John Blatchley and his Crewe-based design team.

longitudinal tubular section and an additional box-section cross-member added into the cruciform bracing. The radius rod provided on the Silver Clouds for rear axle control was deemed unnecessary on the Phantom and was not fitted. All other chassis details were similar to those of the Silver Cloud II and, from the VA series onwards, to those of the Silver Cloud III. As a concession to the vastly larger and heavier coachwork carried and to the likely nature of the cars' use, the rear axle ratio was 3.89:1 as opposed to the 3.08:1 of the V-8 Silver Clouds. This was sufficient to endow the huge Phantom with an extremely creditable performance for

A Park Ward Phantom V. The wheelbase of 12 ft 1 in and overall length of 19 ft 10 in allowed the rear compartment to be unusually spacious without sacrificing luggage capacity or graceful lines. The cabinetwork behind the division incorporated a cocktail cabinet and radio speaker. Switches for the fresh air booster fan, refrigerated air conditioning (optional) and under-seat heater were situated in the right-hand armrest. The radio was located in the left-hand armrest. Electrically operated windows were an option that most purchasers specified. Upholstery for the rear compartment was leather, West of England cloth or other materials to choice, while the front compartment was normally upholstered in leather. The interior design could be varied to suit individual requirements.

Often regarded as the most elegant of the coachwork on the Phantom V was that by James Young Ltd, the very long chassis allowing designer A. F. McNeil's outstanding styling skills to be given free rein. Here we see in the upper photograph his interpretation of the seven-passenger limousine (left), together with the touring limousine, perhaps even more elegant with its closer-coupled body and steeper slope to the tail.

The rare sedanca de ville variant of James Young's touring limousine. This is the 1st Prize winning car at Blenheim Palace, June 1962.

so huge a motor car, with a top speed in excess of 100 mph and acceleration capabilities not far short of those of its smaller stablemates.

What could be termed the 'standard' coachwork on the Phantom V chassis was the Park Ward seven-passenger limousine. This design, with some Mulliner-inspired changes to the upper body panels from October 1962, survived into the 'nineties as the Phantom VI seven-passenger limousine by Mulliner Park Ward. An alternative seven-passenger limousine was offered by James Young Ltd, as well as a closer-coupled touring limousine and, much more rare, a sedanca de ville. As in the case of the Bentley Continental S2, Hooper built only one body on a production Phantom V chassis before ceasing coachbuilding.

In the autumn of 1962 the Silver Cloud III and Bentley S3 were introduced. The most obvious change

to the casual observer was, of course, the twin headlamp arrangement, which was incorporated into an otherwise largely unchanged body style. The changes and improvements introduced for the Silver Cloud III and Bentley S3 went beyond mere external appearance, however, and may be summarised as follows:

- Four-headlamp system for more illumination at a greater distance ahead, and to light more effectively the sides of the road;
- 1½-inch-lower radiator shell with a consequently increased slope to the bonnet for improved forward vision;
- Re-styled front wings without side-lamps let into their tops;
- Flashing indicators and side-lamps combined in a single unit mounted in the noses of the front wings;
- New, smaller bumper overriders (except for North America, and

some coachbuilt cars, for which the older pattern was retained);
- Black leather covering to the fascia capping rail, with token padding;
- Individual front seats (as opposed to the bench-type seat with separate squabs of the Silver Cloud II), designed to give better lateral support for the driver and front-seat passenger;
- A more upright squab and less prominent side padding to the rear seat for more legroom and greater effective width;
- A new Lucas distributor with vacuum advance;
- 9:1 compression ratio for the home market and other countries where 100 octane petrol was readily available (8:1 was retained for export to countries where 100 octane petrol was not available); and
- Larger (2-inch in lieu of 1¾-inch) SU carburetters.

In October 1962 the Silver Cloud III and its sister car the Bentley S3 replaced the Silver Cloud II and Bentley S2. This Silver Cloud III chassis was prepared for exhibition at the 1963 Earls Court Motor Show. The Bentley S3 chassis was identical except for badging and radiator shell.

The appearance of the Silver Cloud III and Bentley S3 standard saloons was unmistakable. The radiator shell was 1½ inches lower than that of their predecessors, and this, together with the horizontally paired headlamps, made for a lower frontal appearance. The side lamps and direction indicators were combined in new units mounted in the noses of the front wings, which meant that the fog lamps no longer needed to double as flashing direction indicators as they had on the I and II. The smaller bumper overriders were new, though the older pattern was retained for North American exports.

The front compartment interior, showing the individual seat cushions and black leather covering to the fascia capping rail. The knob above the windscreen is to turn the radio aerial down parallel with the screen to avoid low garage doorways. The Silver Cloud III and Bentley S3 standard saloon interiors were identical except for the motifs on the instruments and brake pedal pad.

Above: *H. J. Mulliner, by now fully integrated with Park Ward as H. J. Mulliner, Park Ward Ltd, continued to adapt the standard saloon to produce the highly desirable drophead coupé shown for the first year of Silver Cloud III and Bentley S3 production.*

The Bentley S2 Continental drophead coupé designed by V. Koren and built by Park Ward was subsequently developed for the S3 Continental, with paired headlights set at an angle in the extremities of the front wings.

A two-door saloon sharing the same styling was added in 1963.

Opposite and above: In 1963 both the fixed head and drophead variants began to appear on specially adapted Silver Cloud III chassis as well as on the Bentley Continental. The 'Koren Coupés', as they had become known at Park Ward, represented the vast majority of coachbuilt bodies on the Bentley S3 Continental and Silver Cloud III chassis. Though of Park Ward origin, it was the by then combined firm H. J. Mulliner, Park Ward Ltd that built them. The fascia is that of the Silver Cloud III variant. The Bentley Continental S3 differed in having more comprehensive instrumentation, complete with a tachometer.

One hears opposing views as to whether or not the revised frontal appearance was actually in keeping with the superb but rather conservative Silver Cloud body style. From their maker's point of view the change was almost certainly aimed at subtly preparing their customers for the radically new styling of the Silver Shadow that was to follow three years later. However, the fact that the cars sold well at the time and their comparatively buoyant value on today's market both strongly suggest that the frontal appearance was and remains an appealing feature. Other enthusiasts are attracted to the fact that, other than the very limited production Phantoms V and VI, these were the last Rolls-Royce and Bentley cars with a body mounted on a separate chassis. With the same

exceptions, they were also the last to have drum brakes and a live rear axle. These features attracted criticism that Rolls-Royces were old-fashioned, which ignored the fact that other cars of the period, even their supposed rivals, were for the most part dreary and crude in comparison.

The Silver Cloud III came in for merciless criticism in the early 1960s for being supposedly 'old-fashioned'. Motoring journalists drew attention with barely disguised but misdirected contempt to features like the drum brakes, quite ignoring the fact that most other cars of the period also had drum brakes and that the Silver Cloud III's were easily the best drum brakes in the world, if not the best brakes of any kind. To their credit, however, most journalists were prepared to acknowledge that this was a

magnificent motor car that did everything it was designed to do and more, and did it far better than any of its contemporaries. From a purely technical point of view, however, it must be conceded that the Silver Cloud III was beginning to show its age, and in October 1965, when the Silver Shadow was unveiled, the motoring world was amazed by the technical wizardry of it all – what we would call today 'hi-tech'. A quantum leap had been taken and, ultimately, the Silver Shadow went down in history as the most successful Rolls-Royce car of all time. That story, though, belongs in the following chapter.

The Bentley Continental in S3 guise no longer had a more powerful engine or higher gearing than the standard cars, nor did it need to, for

H. J. Mulliner's 'Flying Spur' saloon was continued by H. J. Mulliner, Park Ward Ltd for the S3 Continental. From the 1963 Earls Court Motor Show this extremely handsome car with performance to match also became available on specially modified Silver Cloud III chassis, as seen in the second photograph, though it could be said that the shape blended better with the Bentley radiator with which it was originally conceived than with the Rolls-Royce radiator. It should be noted that the Rolls-Royce version was never designated by its makers as a Continental, despite the prevalent present-day practice of referring to them as such.

Like the H. J. Mulliner and Park Ward designs, James Young coachwork remained unchanged from its previous designs apart from frontal appearance. Again, while this style of coachwork was originally conceived for the Bentley Continental, seen in the first photograph, some examples found their way on to special Silver Cloud III chassis, as seen in the second, for the benefit of those who craved the sleek Continental shape while preferring the Rolls-Royce frontal appearance. Note the door handles, with their characteristic James Young square push-buttons.

A long wheelbase adaptation of the standard saloon continued to be offered in Silver Cloud III and Bentley S3 form. It is shown here with the division with which most such cars were equipped.

James Young accounted for the vast majority of special coachwork on long-wheelbase Silver Cloud III and Bentley S3 chassis, the company's superbly proportioned touring limousine being the dominant design. First introduced for the Silver Cloud II long wheelbase chassis, it was modified with the new frontal appearance for the Silver Cloud III and Bentley S3. In the twilight of their coachbuilding years, James Young had with these cars reached the pinnacle in terms of elegance.

From the Phantom V VA series onwards the Park Ward seven-passenger limousine became the H. J. Mulliner, Park Ward limousine. The panelwork below the waistline remained much as before, but was modified to incorporate the paired headlamps and new side and rear lamp assemblies. From the waistline up, however, all was changed. The windscreen was a different shape, while the formerly rounded rear quarters and boot gave way to razor edges, and the former heavy, painted frames to the door windows disappeared in favour of slim chromium-plated frames. This version of the Phantom V, known within the Company as 'Phantom V½', was aesthetically very pleasing. The design remained essentially unchanged, as the Phantom VI, until 1990, when construction of the final example commenced, making it the longest-lived body design of all time.

The H. J. Mulliner, Park Ward Phantom V State Landaulette. This car was exhibited by Rolls-Royce Ltd at the 1965 Earls Court Motor Show alongside the all-new Silver Shadow. Note that the styling of the boot reverted to that of the original Park Ward design for this model, a pleasing solution to the problem of blending the folding hood with what would otherwise have been a razor-edged boot. The State Landaulette was intended for heads of state and foreign governments.

The James Young seven-passenger and touring limousine designs continued into the VA and later series Phantom V with the frontal styling changes. The above photograph shows the touring limousine, while the right features the seven-passenger limousine, unusually finished in a two-tone colour scheme.

the standard specification was more than adequate to show a clean pair of heels to not only virtually all saloon cars of the period, but also most sports cars! The differences that distinguished the Continental chassis were few and of a minor nature, and it was the coachwork more than anything else that made the Bentley Continentals so special, along with their special comprehensive instrumentation, complete with rev counter. Coachbuilders offering designs for the S3 Continental were down to two surviving firms, and one of these, James Young Ltd, was only destined to last another five years. H. J. Mulliner, Park Ward Ltd offered two-door and four-door saloons and a drophead coupe, all derived from the designs of the two constituent companies.

Several coachbuilt designs were offered on the Silver Cloud III chassis. H. J. Mulliner, Park Ward continued to offer its drophead coupe

adaptation of the standard saloon for the first few months of production, after which a policy decision was made allowing the Bentley Continental body styles to be built on Rolls-Royce Silver Cloud III chassis. Special chassis were built for this purpose with the lower Bentley Continental steering column rake and some other minor Continental features – though the fascias were modified to take the simpler Rolls-Royce instrumentation. James Young followed suit in offering its Continental body styles on the Silver Cloud III chassis. Unfortunately, all this has given rise to the incorrect practice of referring to these coachbuilt Silver Cloud IIIs as 'Continentals', particularly in the UK used car trade. They were never designated as such by their makers.

A long wheelbase chassis was offered and H. J. Mulliner, Park Ward continued to modify the standard saloon bodies to suit it. The long

wheelbase saloon, usually with a division, was 'designed for the owner who requires a limousine car for business use, yet can be used as a saloon at other times'.

Even 30 years on, few cars are as ideally suited to fast, fatigue-free, long distance motoring as a Silver Cloud III or Bentley S3 standard saloon. The lofty driving position and commanding view over the elegant bonnet, smooth but firm ride, a virtually flat floor and beautifully finished interior furnishings and fittings all contribute to the pleasure of driving and a sense of wellbeing. The handling and road-holding, if a little barge-like by modern standards, are nevertheless very good. For the comfort of the back-seat passengers they have few rivals, fewer equals and no betters. Like all Rolls-Royce products they were built to last, so the overwhelming majority of these fine motor cars have survived in good to excellent condition.

TECHNICAL SPECIFICATIONS

Rolls-Royce Silver Cloud II and III, Bentley S2 and S3, Phantom V

Engine

Eight cylinders in 90-degree vee formation, aluminium alloy block with cast iron wet cylinder liners and aluminium cylinder heads.
Bore 4.1 inches (104.14 mm), stroke 3.6 inches (91.44 mm), cubic capacity 380 cu in (6,230 cc).
Overhead valves worked by gear-driven camshaft in vee of engine. Five-bearing crankshaft. Two SU type HD.6 (1¾-inch) carburetters.

1962 (Silver Cloud III, Bentley S3 and Phantom V from VA series): Two SU type HD.8 (2-inch) carburetters.

Chassis

Welded box-section frame with cruciform centre-bracing.

Overall length 17 ft 8 in (5,435 mm) (standard and Bentley Continental), 18 ft 0 in (5,486 mm) (long wheelbase), 19 ft 10 in (6,045 mm) Phantom V.
Wheelbase 10 ft 3 in (3,124 mm) (standard and Bentley Continental), 10 ft 7 in (3,226 mm) (long wheelbase), 12 ft 1 in (3,683 mm) (Phantom V).
Front track 4 ft 10½ in (1,486 mm), 5 ft 0⅞ in (1,546 mm) (Phantom V). Rear track 5 ft 0 in (1,524 mm), 5 ft 4 in (1,625 mm) (Phantom V).

Note: *For overall lengths of Silver Cloud III and Bentley S3, except for North American exports and certain coachbuilt cars, subtract 1 inch (2.5 mm) from the above figures, due to the smaller overriders fitted. This also applies to a small number of* **VA** *series and later Phantom Vs.*

Transmission

Rolls-Royce automatic gearbox and fluid coupling with selector mounted on right of steering column. Four forward speeds and reverse. Ratios: top 1:1, third 1.45:1, second 2.63:1, first 3.82:1, reverse 4.3:1.
Divided propeller shaft with Detroit-type front universal joint, needle roller bearing Hardy-Spicer-type rear universal joint and flexibly mounted centre bearing.
Rear axle: semi-floating type with hypoid bevel gears. Ratio 3.89:1 (standard, long wheelbase and Bentley Continental S2 final series), 2.92:1 (Bentley Continental S2 to chassis **BC99BY**), 3.89:1 (Phantom V).

Steering

Power-assisted cam and roller, Hobourn Eaton belt-driven pump. Three-piece track linkage. Turns, lock to lock, 4¼.

Suspension

Front: independent by coil springs and rubber-bushed wishbones, double-acting hydraulic dampers and anti-roll bar.
Rear: semi-elliptic leaf springs protected by leather gaiters. Controllable hydraulic dampers by solenoid operated by switch on left side of steering column. 'Z'-type axle control rod (except Phantom V).

Brakes

Hydraulic front, hydraulic and mechanical rear, drum brakes. Operation by means of friction disc servo on offside of gearbox, which applies brakes through two master cylinders and dual hydraulic circuits and assists mechanical application of rear brakes. Handbrake on rear wheels by pull-and-twist handle under fascia through cable and mechanical linkage. Cast iron drums.

Chassis lubrication system

Long-life grease lubrication by nipples at 21 points.

Fuel system

Rear-mounted petrol tank, capacity 18 gallons (21.6 US gallons, 81.8 litres) (Phantom V 23 gallons (27.6 US gallons, 105 litres). Twin SU electric fuel pump mounted in frame.

Road wheels and tyres

15-inch steel disc wheels on five studs, carrying 8.20 x 15 tyres (Phantom V 8.90 x 15 tyres).

CHASSIS AND ENGINE NUMBERS

Silver Cloud II

Chassis sub-series starting with 1 use odd numbers only, omitting 13. Those starting with 2 use even numbers only.

Chassis numbers	Year
SPA2-362, SRA1-325	1959-1960
STB2-500, SVB1-501	1960
SWC2-730, SXC1-671	1960-61
SYD2-550, SZD1-551	1961
SAE1-685	1961-62

Total: 2,418 cars.

Bentley S2

Chassis sub-series starting with 1 use odd numbers only, omitting 13. Those starting with 2 use even numbers only.

Chassis numbers	Year
B1AA-B325AA, B2AM-B326AM	1959-60
B1BR-B501BR, B2BS-B500BS	1960
B1CT-B445CT, B2CU-B756CU	1960-61
B1DV-B501DV, B2DW-B376DW	1961-62

Total: 1,863 cars.

Silver Cloud II long wheelbase

Chassis are numbered consecutively, omitting 13.

Chassis numbers	Year
LCA1-76	1959-60
LCB1-101	1960-61
LCC1-101	1961-62
LCD1-25	1962

Total: 299 cars.

Bentley S2 long wheelbase

Chassis are numbered consecutively, omitting 13.

Series	Chassis numbers	Year
A	LBA1-26	1960
B	LBB1-33	1961-1962

Total: 57 cars.

Bentley Continental S2

Chassis are numbered consecutively, omitting 13.

Chassis numbers	Year
BC1AR-BC151AR	1959-60
BC1BY-BC101BY	1960-61
BC1CZ-BC139CZ	1961-62

Total: 388 cars.

Phantom V

Chassis series and sub-series starting with 1 use odd numbers only, omitting 13. Those starting with 2 use even numbers only.

Chassis numbers	Year
5AS1-5AS101, 5AT2-5AT100	1959-61
5BV1-5BV101, 5BX2-5BX100	1961-62
5CG1-5CG79	1961-62
5VA1-5VA123	1962-64
5VB1-5VB51	1963-64
5VC1-5VC51	1964
5VD1-5VD101	1964-65
5VE1-5VE51	1965-66
5VF1-5VF183	1966-68

Total: 516 cars.

Silver Cloud III

All chassis series start with 1 and use odd numbers only, omitting 13.

Chassis numbers	Year
SAZ1-61	1962
B series was omitted	
SCX1-877	1962-63
SDW1-601	1963
SEV1-495	1963-64
SFU1-803	1963-64
SGT1-659	1964
SHS1-357	1964-65
SJR1-623	1965
SKP1-423	1965
CSC1B-CSC141B (coachbuilt)	1965
CSC1C-CSC83C (coachbuilt)	1965-66

Total: 2,556 cars.

Bentley S3

All chassis series start with 2 and use even numbers only.

Chassis numbers	Year
B2AV-B26AV	1962
'B' series was omitted	
B2CN-B828CN	1962-63
B2DF-B198DF	1963
B2EC-B530EC	1963-64
B2FG-B350FG	1964
B2GJ-B200GJ	1964-65
B2HN-B400HN	1965
B2JP-B40JP	1965

Total: 1,286 cars.

Silver Cloud III long wheelbase

All chassis series start with 1 and use odd numbers only, omitting 13.

Chassis numbers	Year
CAL1-83	1962-63
CBL1-61	1963
CCL1-101	1963-64
CDL1-95	1964
CEL1-105	1964-65
CFL1-41	1965
CGL1-29	1965

Total: 254 cars.

Bentley S3 long wheelbase

All chassis series start with 2 and use even numbers only.

Chassis numbers	Year
BAL2-30	1962-63
BBL2-12	1964-65
BCL2-22	1965

Total: 32 cars.

Bentley Continental S3

All chassis series start with 2 and use even numbers only.

Chassis numbers	Year
BC2XA-BC174XA	1962-63
BC2XB-BC100XB	1963
BC2XC-BC202XC	1963-65
BC2XD-BC28XD	1965
BC2XE-BC120XC	1965-66

Total: 311 cars.

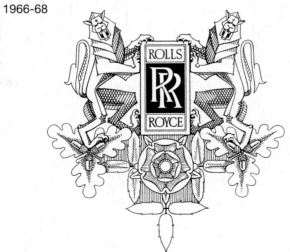

Chapter Eight

A radically new Rolls-Royce

'*The Rolls-Royce and Bentley have been fundamentally redesigned. All that they now have in common with the cars they replace is the recently introduced (and now modified) 6,230 cc eight-cylinder power unit. Why this radical change? Because nothing less could fully translate Rolls-Royce motoring into the terms of heavy traffic and modern roads.*

'*The Silver Shadow and Bentley T Series will cruise at high speeds in silence and with complete safety and controllability. They can be driven very fast even over rough, steeply cambered European roads. And yet they have every quality that fits a car for the life of a modern city: effortless handling and flexibility in traffic, great comfort, swift and simple parking.*

'*This kind of all-round performance requires the full use of the most modern automotive technology. But for Rolls-Royce performance can never be enough. It is the manner of the performance that counts. That is why ten years of intensive development have gone into making all independent suspension, automatic height control, power disc brakes, power steering and automatic transmission work to Rolls-Royce standards.*

'*In short: these cars combine advanced engineering and safety specifications with traditional Rolls-Royce standards of craftsmanship. In the manner of their performance they are as revolutionary as the Silver Ghost was 59 years ago.*'

(Rolls-Royce Ltd's announcement of the Silver Shadow and Bentley T Series cars in the 8 October 1965 edition of *The Autocar*).

Among the most important considerations in the styling of the Silver Shadow was that it should be modern and able to withstand the ravages of time. Obviously a firm such as Rolls-Royce, with a relatively modest output, cannot afford the luxury of frequent styling changes. Therefore styling features that are liable to date quickly need to be avoided. The body style that resulted from these aims and constraints was fairly conservative but quite timeless. It is difficult for the untrained eye to date a Silver Shadow or T Series at a glance, and they do not look unduly dated even today.

Though the Silver Shadow and Bentley T Series were smaller overall than their predecessors, being 6¾ inches shorter, 4½ inches lower and 3¾ inches narrower, they made more efficient use of the available space. They were considerably roomier inside and the boot was both bigger and more conveniently shaped. However, to the owner accustomed to the earlier cars, much that was familiar remained. The violin key-style switches, which worked better than those of any other car, were familiar in both appearance and location, while the steering wheel had the same rim section and diameter as that of the Silver Cloud III, though now with two spokes instead of three as a concession to modern trends. A major improvement was the positioning of the speedometer and other instruments directly in front of the driver.

Beneath the relatively conservative

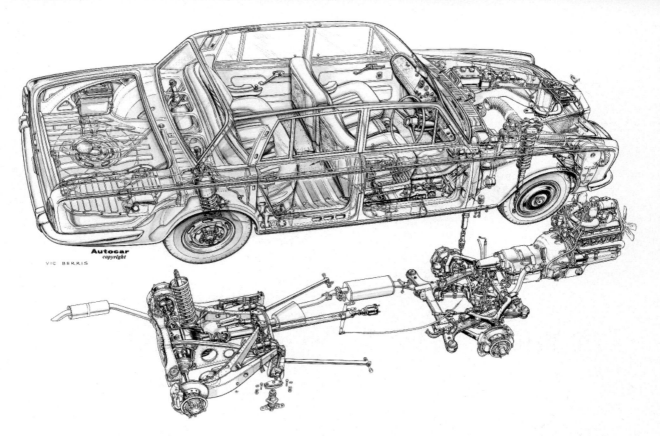

Autocar
copyright

VIC BERRIS

The Silver Shadow was the first Rolls-Royce car to employ unitary, or monocoque, construction. This mode of construction is chassisless and relies upon the stiffness of the actual body shell for its rigidity, which is superior to that of the best separate-chassis construction. The Silver Shadow had a front sub-frame of closed box-section construction carrying the engine/gearbox unit and front suspension, and a separate rear sub-frame supporting the final drive and independent rear suspension components.

The Silver Shadow and Bentley T Series standard saloons, though having some subtle styling features and fittings in common with their predecessors the Silver Cloud III and S3, were a vast departure from those tall, elegantly sculptured cars. One thing that did not change was the quality of build, materials, fittings and finish, all of which were of a high order. They were a runaway success and three decades later are still extremely impressive cars.

For the seasoned Rolls-Royce or Bentley driver and passenger there was much that was familiar in the Silver Shadow and T Series – vast areas of the finest Connolly hide, beautiful burr walnut veneers and deep-pile Wilton carpet with hide edge binding. Many of the switches and fittings, too, were little changed from the Silver Cloud III and the steering wheel was of the same size and rim section, though now with two spokes instead of three. The separate front seats were electrically operated for reach and height/cushion tilt adjustments by means of two eight-way switches mounted between the seat cushions.

exterior lay a technical specification that was second to none for sophistication and innovation. When first introduced in 1965 these cars were easily the most technically advanced in the world. In fact, the same overall design concept still forms the basis of the current range of cars.

Unlike their predecessors, the Silver Shadow series had no separate chassis, the extremely rigid monocoque body being mounted on front and rear sub-frames that carried the engine, gearbox, front suspension and steering equipment and rear axle and rear suspension respectively. Suspension was all-independent with front anti-dive and rear anti-lift characteristics to resist nose-diving under heavy braking. Superimposed on the suspension, but playing no part in the actual springing or damping, was a sophisticated high-pressure hydraulic self-levelling, or height control, system to maintain optimum ride height and attitude regardless of load and load distribution. This system operated at two speeds, fast levelling taking effect when a door was open or

neutral selected. The hydraulic pressure for the levelling and brakes was (and still is on current models) supplied by a pair of camshaft-driven piston pumps and stored in spherical accumulators. Rams above each coil spring were supplied with hydraulic fluid under pressure by height control valves, or sensors, one for the front pair of rams and two for the rear pair.

The four-wheel disc brake system incorporated two independent powered circuits, using high-pressure hydraulics from the same pump and accumulator that supplied the height control system for one circuit, the second pump and accumulator for the second circuit, with a third, conventional master cylinder circuit connected directly to the pedal. The master cylinder circuit served the same purpose as the mechanical linkage in the old brake system, ie to introduce positive 'feel' into the pedal. A deceleration-conscious pressure-limiting valve, or 'G-valve', was provided to prevent premature wheel locking.

Power-assisted steering was by a Saginaw (US) recirculating ball

steering box with integral ram – as opposed to the external ram of the Silver Cloud/S Series system – supplied with hydraulic pressure by a Hobourn Eaton (later Saginaw) belt-driven pump. For the first time on a Rolls-Royce or Bentley the steering column was collapsible, for safety.

The engine used for the Silver Shadow series was, at first, basically the same 6,230 cc unit first introduced in October 1959, though with redesigned cylinder heads that gave a more efficient combustion chamber shape and brought the spark plugs up to a more readily accessible position above the redesigned exhaust manifolds. Likewise, the automatic gearbox was still the four-speed Rolls-Royce box with fluid coupling as first introduced in 1952, though with aluminium alloy in lieu of cast iron for the main casing and some internal parts and with a freewheel incorporated for first and second gears – this feature being inoperative with '2' selected in order to provide engine braking when required. Cars for North America, however, had a

James Young Ltd, whose coachbuilding activities ceased in 1968 when the last of its magnificent Phantom Vs was delivered, briefly turned its hand to the Silver Shadow and Bentley T Series with a series of 50 two-door saloons (35 Silver Shadows, 15 Bentleys) adapted from standard saloon body shells. The rebuilding as two-door cars included the elimination of the chromium waist embellisher and the fitting of the distinctive James Young door handles, seating and interior woodwork.

The H. J. Mulliner, Park Ward Two-door Saloon was more distinctively styled than the James Young version. The steeply raked windscreen, the traditional but sleek wingline and details like the H. J. Mulliner-pattern door handles all add flair to this graceful and enduring design. Here we see design draughtsman Peter Wharton's original coloured wash drawing, and the reality.

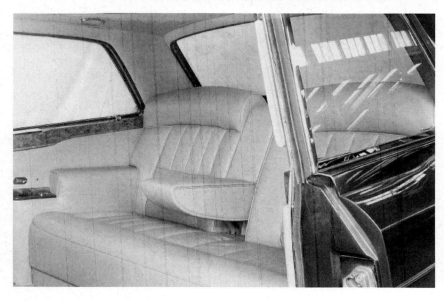

The interior views of the H. J. Mulliner, Park Ward two-door saloon show the distinctive seating and other details. The fascia shared the Standard Saloon layout but the centre panel stood out slightly from the surrounding areas and flame-pattern veneers with pale crossbanding added an extra air of quality to these coachbuilt cars. Note the separate armchair-like seats for the rear passengers.

In September 1967 a drophead coupé variant of the H. J. Mulliner, Park Ward coachbuilt car was introduced. The hood was power-operated by means of an electric motor driving an hydraulic pump, with hydraulic rams. The stowed hood and its operating mechanism infringed on luggage space to a considerable degree and the rear seat was of necessity narrower than that of the Two-door Saloon, none of which detracted seriously from the extreme desirability of this fine convertible. Just how enduring a design this proved to be is demonstrated by the fact that the last of these fine convertibles were being built just as this book went to press, having been marketed as the Corniche since 1971 and called Corniche IV in its latest technically highly sophisticated form.

three-speed automatic transmission with torque converter, bought in complete from General Motors in Detroit and fitted unmodified – such was the state of the art of automatic transmission manufacture in the US. In both cases, range selection was electrically operated, thus eliminating a possible noise path and providing light fingertip action.

As a subsidiary of Rolls-Royce Ltd, H. J. Mulliner, Park Ward was best placed to fulfil the demand for coachbuilt cars, even if they were no longer really coachbuilt in the previously accepted sense. Apart from 50 cars from James Young and a single car from Pininfarina, the task

In May 1969 the Silver Shadow Long Wheelbase Saloon, with or without division, was introduced. This variant was 4 inches longer than the standard saloon aft of the centre pillars. The backlight was smaller, though the standard rear glass was sometimes specified, particularly on cars without division, and an Everflex-covered roof often distinguished these cars.

Heavy padding and lots of leather replaced the cabinetwork previously associated with division-equipped cars. This was at the height of a flurry of passive safety legislation in the United States, which also gave rise to the revised fascia, recessed door handles and other interior details shown, which applied to all models in the range.

In March 1971, within two weeks of the Company going into receivership, just to show that it was 'business as usual' in the Car Division, a new model was announced. More accurately, an existing model had been significantly revised and given a distinctive new model name. The H. J. Mulliner, Park Ward coachbuilt Silver Shadow and T Series cars became the Corniche. Here are the Rolls-Royce Corniche two-door saloon and the much rarer Bentley version, the latter shown with the optional 'Everflex' roof covering.

The Corniche fascia was all new, with comprehensive instrumentation including a tachometer. The 15-inch wood-rimmed steering wheel with leather-covered spokes was a short-lived casualty of the emerging safety consciousness, and the standard Silver Shadow wheel was quickly substituted.

It was the Convertible version of the Corniche (it was no longer marketed as a 'drophead coupé') that really captured the imagination. 'The name Corniche has been chosen for the latest coachbuilt models because it symbolises their high cruising speeds and their ability to cover great distances with the minimum of fatigue for driver and passengers,' announced the Company.

of turning out sleek new two-door saloon and drophead coupé designs for the new models fell to the in-house coachbuilder. These cars, like the standard saloon, were designed by John Blatchley's styling team at Crewe and were built in a manner that was more body engineering than coachbuilding, though the interior trimming and finishing remained traditional coachbuilding tasks. They were built on special base units supplied by Pressed Steel Fisher of Cowley, using panels supplied in roughly finished form by outside suppliers. They formed the basis of what was to become the Corniche.

Initially there was no long wheelbase version of the Silver Shadow. The chassisless construction appears to have been the main stumbling block, though the solution eventually adopted – cutting a standard body shell in half and letting in an extra 4 inches just aft of the centre pillars – was remarkably simple and worked well. As had been the case with long wheelbase versions of the Silver Cloud long wheelbase saloons, this work was carried out at the Willesden works of H. J. Mulliner, Park Ward Ltd. After being modified to long wheelbase specification, the body shells were transported to Crewe where they were fed on to the production line for finishing, either with or without a division.

During the 15-year production run of the Silver Shadow and its derivatives, over 2,000 individual technical and coachwork changes were introduced, culminating in the introduction of the Silver Shadow II range in February 1977; the more notable of these are outlined in the technical specification. Perhaps the most important change, apart from those that came with the Silver Shadow II range, was the enlargement of the engine capacity from 6,230 cc to 6,750 cc, by lengthening the stroke from 3.6 to 3.9 inches; this took place in July 1970. The increase in power output that could reasonably have been expected to result from this change was largely absorbed by the exhaust emission control equipment

that was required to be fitted, firstly on cars for California and later for the remainder of North America and other countries, notably Australia and Japan. The three-speed GM automatic transmission fitted to North American delivery cars began to appear on cars for other markets during 1968 and was standard by November of that year.

In 1970 the aero engine side of the business found itself in difficulties over the runaway development costs of the RB.211 jet engine for the new generation of wide-bodied airliners. However, the Car Division, ironically enough, had become profitable in its own right, thanks to the success of the Silver Shadow, and became a separate company, Rolls-Royce Motors Ltd, in 1971. Meanwhile the aero business was nationalised, though it has since been re-privatised and is now Rolls-Royce PLC.

To have announced a new model just after the Company had been placed in the hands of the official receiver over financial problems associated with the RB.211 jet engine project demonstrated just how confident and forward-looking the Car Division remained. This confidence was well founded. The Division was completely solvent, profitable and, furthermore, its instructions from the receiver were quite specific – business as usual. So, early in March 1971 the Corniche was unveiled. It was not so much a new model as a significantly revised existing one. With a new low-loss exhaust system, bolder radiator shell (half an inch deeper, measured front to back), new fascia, new spun stainless steel wheel trims and 'Corniche' badging, the H. J. Mulliner, Park Ward two-door cars had a new lease of life that only very recently came to an end. The name Corniche was taken from an area around Nice, where the Grand Corniche road winds spectacularly around the Mediterranean coast – a place in which a car like the Corniche comes very much into its own.

Modifications to the valve and ignition timing, a more efficient air intake silencer and a larger-bore, low-

loss exhaust system all contributed to the increased performance of the Corniche over that of the standard Silver Shadow models. Traditionally, Rolls-Royce does not disclose the power output of its motor car engines, preferring to describe it as 'adequate' or 'sufficient'. However, in the case of the Corniche it was a case of 'adequate plus 10 per cent'; sufficiently adequate, in fact, to give the big coupés a top speed in excess of 120 mph, with acceleration capabilities, particularly from speeds above 50 mph, considerably better than those of the standard car, itself no sluggard, and indeed better than those of many sports cars of the period! The engine modifications did not apply to the Corniche for export to the United States, due to the need to comply with the more stringent emission regulations in that country.

The drophead coupé version of the Corniche, which was actually marketed as the Convertible, using the American terminology, is surely the ultimate in high-performance open-air motoring. It has been so successful that it remained a current model until the end of 1994, with deliveries continuing into 1995.

In March 1975 a second luxurious two-door coachbuilt car was added to the range. This was the Pininfarina-styled Camargue – a name that, like Corniche, has its origins in the South of France, a part of the world with close associations with Sir Henry Royce, who carried out much of his design work at his winter home 'La Villa Mimosa' at Le Canadel. The name Camargue is derived from the Ile de la Camargue, in the delta of the Rhone on the Mediterranean coast.

In October 1969 the Italian stylist had been commissioned to design a car that would be suitable for production by H. J. Mulliner, Park Ward and that could be based upon the standard mechanical units and base platform of the Silver Shadow. It was specified that the car should be a two-door saloon offering superior passenger and luggage accommodation to the then current Silver Shadow two-door saloon.

During its 15-year production run the Silver Shadow and Bentley T Series underwent a continuous programme of changes, both mechanical and coachwork. The cars illustrated here have such later features as ventilated wheel covers, more boldly flared wheel arches, three-speed automatic transmission (standard from the outset on cars for North America), compliant front suspension and 6,750 cc engine. The interior view shows the 'TV screen'-style warning lights introduced in September 1972 as part of a major electrical system revision.

Code-named 'Delta' within the Company, the Camargue was announced in March 1975. Like the Corniche it was built on the Silver Shadow floor pan from welded steel pressings with aluminium doors and boot and bonnet lids. The Camargue's styling, by Sergio Pininfarina, was quite different from that of any Rolls-Royce that had come before it. In detail, too, it was in a class apart, with its special seats, distinctive aircraft-style fascia and the world's first fully automatic split-level air conditioning system.

David (later Sir David) Plastow was the first Managing Director of Rolls-Royce Motors Ltd, the company formed when the former Motor Car Division separated from the aero engine side of Rolls-Royce Ltd in 1971. After the merger with Vickers in 1980 Sir David became Chairman and Managing Director of that group. He is seen here with a Camargue outside the main entrance to the Crewe factory office block, where the reception area now stands.

The Camargue was the first model designed on a metric basis. Its styling was characteristically Pininfarina and the car looks much larger than the Corniche, though in fact it was the same length but 3.9 inches wider. The deep, steeply raked windscreen and rear window and curved side windows helped give the Camargue a strikingly rakish appearance.

At first, construction of the Camargue was divided between Crewe and Mulliner Park Ward in London, with the cars being transported backwards and forwards between the two plants for the various operations. However, in 1976, with world demand for the coachbuilt models soaring, a decision was reached to transfer Camargue production to Crewe in order to relieve the pressure from the overloaded Mulliner Park Ward Division, which was then producing the Corniche and Phantom VI as well as the Camargue. Production of the Camargue at Crewe, on a special line, commenced in the summer of 1978.

A major innovation in keeping with the established Rolls-Royce Motors policy of using low-volume coachbuilt models as the technical leaders of the range was the fully automatic, split-level air conditioning system. This was designed and developed by Rolls-Royce Motors engineers and, as the first and only such system to offer completely independent automatic temperature control at two levels, it was, and remains, the most advanced available. Once the desired temperatures for the upper and lower parts of the interior have been set, the car may be driven from the Arctic Circle to the Equator without the need to adjust the controls, and the selected temperatures are maintained automatically and unobtrusively. The ultimate 'set and forget' system.

The pricing of the Camargue was, from its inception, set at 50 per cent above that of the Corniche and 35 per cent more even than the huge hand-built Phantom VI, not because it cost that much more to build but merely to ensure its exclusivity as the Rolls-Royce flagship, and to make the point

that Rolls-Royce Motors Ltd fully intended remaining at the very pinnacle of the luxury car pyramid.

The most significant changes to the Silver Shadow range of cars occurred in February 1977. These changes to the technical specification and appearance were considered sufficient to justify the revised model designations Silver Shadow II and Bentley T2. The policy of bestowing individual model names to body styles rather than to chassis types was extended to the long wheelbase version of the standard car, which became the Silver Wraith II, in honour of the first post-war Rolls-Royce.

The changes introduced in a single package for these Series II cars affected the external appearance, interior, mechanical specification and handling characteristics of the car. Dealing with each in turn, the changes most obvious to the observer in the street were the adoption as standard of American-style, wrap-around, black polyurethane-faced bumpers, a deeper (front to back) radiator shell like that of the Corniche and the fitting of an 'air dam' below the front bumper. These Silver Shadow II recognition points did not apply in the United States, partly because the bumpers and deeper radiator shell were already familiar on US export Silver Shadows and partly because the air dam was not fitted to Silver Shadow IIs for that market, so Americans had to rely for identification on the 'SILVER SHADOW II' badge on the boot lid and the new fascia.

The most immediately noticeable interior change was that the Silver Shadow II range of cars reverted to having a full set of instruments and a suitably impressive fascia in which to mount them. Actually, the new fascia had appeared a year or so earlier, without fanfare, on the Corniche.

More important than the cosmetic changes were the new technical features of the Silver Shadow II range, and perhaps the most significant of these, from the point of view of the enthusiastic driver, was the rack-and-pinion steering. At

speed, with its highly refined power assistance, as well as being more precise and sensitive, it provided the positive 'feel' that experienced drivers expect. A still smaller (15-inch) steering wheel went with the new steering system. Modifications to the front suspension geometry, designed to keep the front wheels more upright when cornering, improved responsiveness still further while reducing roll angles.

There were also some power-unit changes, mainly in the cooling and carburation areas. A smaller but more efficient seven-bladed plastic fan, driven through a viscous coupling, was assisted by a thermostatically controlled electric fan mounted forward of the radiator.

The large SU type HD.8 carburetters were replaced with the much more technically advanced, though slightly smaller, HIF.7s. Their advanced design provided much more efficient maintenance of exhaust emission control standards and, in conjunction with the lower power absorption characteristics of the revised cooling arrangements and a new low-loss twin exhaust system, helped improve fuel economy. The twin stainless steel exhaust system also compensated for the slight loss of power incurred by the smaller carburetters. The alternator was of increased capacity and the oil filter was now the modern disposable spin-on type in lieu of the earlier separate-element type.

The highly sophisticated automatic bi-level air conditioning system, first introduced on the Camargue and adopted for the Corniche for 1976, was standard on all models in the Silver Shadow II range of cars.

By 1967, with the chassis-less Silver Shadow firmly established, the last independent coachbuilding firm, James Young Ltd, was winding down its operations, leaving H. J. Mulliner, Park Ward Ltd, a Rolls-Royce subsidiary, as the only remaining coachbuilder. The Phantom V chassis remained as the only Rolls-Royce chassis on which true coachbuilt bodies in the traditional sense could be built. This meant that the Phantom

Sufficient new features were introduced at the same time on the Silver Shadow and T Series cars for deliveries commencing February 1977 to justify new model designations. Hence the Silver Shadow II and Bentley T2, and, for the first time, a distinctive name for the long wheelbase car, named Silver Wraith II. Externally, the obvious changes were black polyurethane-faced bumpers (already seen on US export cars from mid-1973) and an air dam under the front bumper (not fitted to US exports). Also the radiator was increased in front to back measurement by 15 per cent to present a bolder, more massive appearance, like that of the Corniche. The headlamp wash/wipe facility, seen in the front view of the Silver Shadow II, was introduced in June 1978, but again this did not apply for the US market. The Silver Wraith II in the second photograph was further distinguished from its shorter wheelbase stablemate by the fitting of Corniche/Camargue-pattern wheel trims.

By the time the Silver Shadow II appeared, the Company's efforts at providing a Bentley alternative had become a little half-hearted. The name on the engine rocker covers was Rolls-Royce, the chassis number was stamped on a Rolls-Royce maker's plate and the instruments on the fascia carried the 'entwined-Rs' logo. In spite of this, demand for the Bentley would not go away and a remarkable Bentley resurgence was just around the corner. The headlamp wash/wipe facility seen here was introduced on all models in the Silver Shadow II range, except those for North America, from June 1978.

Inside the Silver Shadow II family of cars, the only obvious change was the all-new fascia. A four-in-one instrument was positioned in front of the driver alongside the new electronic speedometer. The controls for the automatic air conditioning system can be seen to the left of the steering column, while those for the electronic speed control were now incorporated in the gear selector stalk on the right. The seating and other interior details (other than the fascia) remained unchanged from those of earlier Silver Shadows. The generous legroom and narrow rear window indicate that this is the long-wheelbase variant.

For 1977 the polyurethane-faced bumpers of the Silver Shadow II were also applied to the coachbuilt Corniche. The new fascia and automatic air conditioning had actually been incorporated into this model for the 1976 season. However, the model designation 'Corniche II' was not applied until 1987 (United States) and 1988 (other markets).

The Phantom VI, in its earliest form, was basically a Phantom V fitted with separate front and rear air conditioning units, a revised fascia similar to that of the early Silver Shadows and the Silver Shadow-type 6,230 cc engine. The first Phantom VI was delivered on 1 January 1969. The only external recognition feature of the earliest cars was that the bonnet lids were shorter than those of a Phantom V, to allow the fitting of a Silver Shadow-type air conditioning intake grille in the scuttle top.

However, from 1972 more changes began to appear, starting with the rear compartment door being hinged at the front instead of at the rear. This and other changes such as burst-proof locks and a collapsible steering column were incorporated to comply with European safety legislation.

Not all Phantom VIs were limousines. The State Landaulette, of which four were built on Phantom V chassis, was also available as a Phantom VI. It is worth noting again that the very early rounded style of Park Ward boot was retained for this design, as opposed to the razor-edged boot of the later limousines.

was now a purely H. J. Mulliner, Park Ward motor car. This, together with the decision to use the 6,230 cc Silver Shadow engine and fit as standard separate air conditioning systems for front and rear compartments, led to the designation Phantom VI being applied from 1968.

The earliest Phantom VIs could be externally distinguished from an H. J. Mulliner, Park Ward Phantom V only by the opening panels of the bonnet being slightly shorter to make room for an air intake grille on the scuttle top and by turn indicator repeaters on the sides of the front wings. Inside, the only obvious difference was the flat fascia with padded capping rail along similar lines to that of the early Silver Shadows. This change was due to the fitting of the efficient Silver Shadow-type air conditioning system with its swivelling outlets on the fascia, which also explains the new grille in the scuttle.

From 1972 Phantom VIs began to appear with front-hinged doors to the rear compartment. This was to satisfy new European safety legislation, which also required burst-proof door locks, a collapsible steering column and a more effective handbrake, all of which were incorporated successfully. At around the same time, some subtle changes to the external body details began to appear, including the stainless steel sill embellisher being extended over the wheel arches.

Interestingly, the task of constructing the Phantom VI chassis was transferred in August 1973 to Mulliner Park Ward in London. Thus the coachbuilder became the builder of the complete car, though of course the mechanical units still came from Crewe.

The basically Phantom V mechanical specification, including the four-speed fluid coupling automatic gearbox and mechanical friction-disc servo for the brakes, remained intact on the Phantom VI until the spring of 1978, when a number of significant changes were introduced. These brought the Phantom more into line with the Silver Shadow range in that the 6,750

cc engine, GM400 three-speed automatic transmission and high-pressure hydraulics for the braking system were all adopted. The change to the braking system was made necessary by the fact that the gearbox rear extension that carried the cross-shaft for the mechanical servo was incompatible with the General Motors transmission. Thus the friction-disc servo that in one form or another had served in Rolls-Royce cars so well since 1924 at last gave way to the thoroughly modern system of the Silver Shadow, though for various technical reasons it was not practical to fit the Phantom with disc brakes.

Despite these changes and the fitting of centralised door and boot locking and the like, the Phantom VI remained very much a 1950s design. It is therefore all the more remarkable that there was still a sufficiently healthy demand to justify keeping it in production much longer than the most optimistic forecast. Its longevity is a tribute to the original design.

TECHNICAL SPECIFICATIONS

Rolls-Royce Silver Shadow, Bentley T Series and derivative models

Engine

Eight cylinders in 90-degree vee formation, aluminium alloy block with cast iron wet cylinder liners and aluminium cylinder heads.
Bore 4.1 inches (104.14 mm), stroke 3.6 inches (91.44 mm), cubic capacity 380 cu in (6,230 cc). Overhead valves worked by gear-driven camshaft in vee of engine. Five-bearing crankshaft. Two SU type HD.8 (2-inch) carburetters.

1970: Stroke 3.9 inches (99.1 mm), cubic capacity 412 cu in (6,750 cc).
1975 (home market Camargue and Corniche): Solex type 4A1 four-barrel downdraught carburetter.
1977 (Silver Shadow II range): Two

SU type HIF.7 (1⅞-inch) carburetters.
1980 (California): Lucas K-Jetronic fuel injection.

Chassis

Monocoque construction with separate front and rear sub-frames:
Front – steel box-section construction mounted to car underframe by resilient metal mounts.
Rear – comprises final drive cross-member mounted to underframe by two resilient metal mounts and connected by torque reaction arm to rear sub-frame. Short telescopic damper fitted to each front mount to dampen fore and aft movement.
Overall length 16 ft 11½ in (5,169 mm) (standard), 17 ft 3½ in (5,270 mm) (long wheelbase), 17 ft 0½ in (5,194 mm) (Silver Shadow II), 17 ft 4½ in (5,296 mm) (Silver Wraith II).
Wheelbase 9 ft 11½ in (3,035 mm) (standard), 10 ft 3½ in (3,137 mm) (long wheelbase).
Track, front and rear 4 ft 9½ in (1,460 mm)

Transmission

Cars for other than North America: Rolls-Royce automatic gearbox and fluid coupling with selector mounted on right of steering column. Four forward speeds and reverse. Ratios: top 1:1, third 1.45:1, second 2.63:1, first 3.82:1, reverse 4.3:1.
Cars for North America: General Motors GM400 three-speed automatic transmission and torque converter. Ratios: top 1:1, third 1.5:1, first 2.5:1, reverse 2:1.

1968: GM400 three-speed automatic transmission all cars.

One-piece propeller shaft.
Final drive: hypoid bevel rigidly mounted on cross-member which in turn is mounted to body underframe by resilient metal mounts. Drive transmitted to rear wheels by two drive shafts. Inner end of each shaft is connected to final drive by Detroit-type ball and trunnion joint and outer

end by Hardy-Spicer-type universal joint. Ratio 3.08:1.

Steering

Power-assisted recirculating ball, Hobourn Eaton belt-driven pump. Three-piece track linkage. Turns, lock to lock, 4.

1967: Saginaw pump.
1968: Higher steering ratio.
1971: Steering ratio increased further.
1977 (Silver Shadow II range): Power-assisted rack-and-pinion steering with centre take-off.

Suspension

Front: independent by coil springs and rubber-bushed wishbones, double-acting hydraulic telescopic dampers and anti-roll bar.
Rear: independent by coil springs and trailing arms, hydraulic telescopic dampers.

From serial number 12734 (Corniche) and 13485 (all cars): Compliant front suspension.

Hydraulic system

Two camshaft-driven hydraulic pumps delivering brake fluid under pressure (up to 2,500 psi) to pair of hydraulic accumulators mounted on side of crankcase. Hydraulic pressure stored in accumulators used for braking and height control systems. Two low-pressure warning lights on fascia, one for each hydraulic circuit.

Height control system

Fully automatic hydraulic height control system to maintain standing height of car under all load conditions, by means of height control valves and hydraulic rams over coil spring of each wheel. This system was designed to operate at two speeds – slow levelling when driving and fast levelling with gear selector lever in neutral or door opened.

1969: Front height control deleted.

Brakes

11-inch disc brakes on all four wheels. Each front wheel fitted with two twin-cylinder callipers and each rear wheel with one four-cylinder calliper. Three separate and independent hydraulic circuits, two from high-pressure hydraulic system operated by distribution valves connected to brake pedal and direct master cylinder circuit. Deceleration-conscious, pressure-limiting valve ('G' valve) incorporated in master cylinder circuit on very early cars (later moved to one of power circuits) to prevent premature rear wheel locking. Separate brake pads for handbrake.

1975: Master cylinder circuit deleted.

Chassis lubrication system

Long-life grease lubrication.

Fuel system

Rear-mounted petrol tank, capacity 24 gallons (29 US gallons, 109 litres). Twin SU electric fuel pump mounted in body underframe.

Road wheels and tyres

15-inch steel disc wheels on five studs, carrying 8.45 x 15 tyres. Compliant front suspension cars: 205 x 15 radial ply tyres, later 235/70 x 15.

CHASSIS NUMBERING SYSTEM

Silver Shadow and derivative models

In October 1965, when the Silver Shadow and Bentley T Series cars were introduced, a changed system of numbering was adopted. Within these Car Serial Numbers, each digit of the three-letter prefix has a specific meaning, explained below. This prefix is followed by a four- or five-digit number. The Car Serial Number shown as the example below is that of the first Silver Shadow series car, which was actually a Bentley T Series. It should be noted that the Silver Shadow numbering system included the derivative Corniche and Camargue models and was also adopted for the Phantom VI.

S	B	H	1	0	0	1
1	2	3	4	5	6	7

1 = body type
   S – Saloon
   C – Coachbuilt (including Drophead Coupé cars prior to car number 6646)
   D – Drophead Coupé (or Convertible) from 6646
   L – Long Wheelbase
   J – Camargue
   P – Phantom VI

2 = marque
   R – Rolls-Royce
   B – Bentley

3 = steering position/year
   H – home (right-hand drive)
   X – export (left-hand drive)

On North American specification cars, commencing with the 1972 model year, X was replaced by a year code letter as follows:

   A – 1972
   B – 1973
   C – 1974
   D – 1975
   E – 1976
   F – 1977
   G – 1978
   K – 1979
   L – 1980

4-7 = sequential identification number (later five digits)

Cars for California with fuel injection (from 1980) had a 'C' suffix. The numbers following the three-letter prefix began with 1001 in 1965 and ended at 26708 in 1976 (with gaps), then re-commenced with 30001 (Silver Shadow II range, 1977), ending at 41686 in 1980.
The Corniche and Camargue cars with the mineral oil hydraulic system were numbered 50001-50776.

Chapter Nine

The 'eighties and beyond

In October 1980 Rolls-Royce Motors merged with Vickers to become the biggest member of a large and financially secure group of companies. Sir David Plastow, who had been the first (and only) Managing Director of the independent Rolls-Royce Motors Ltd, became Chairman and Managing Director of Vickers PLC. Within days of the merger a new range of cars, comprising the Silver Spirit, Silver Spur (long wheelbase) and Bentley Mulsanne, was announced. The Corniche Convertible and Camargue were retained from the previous Silver Shadow range, though the Corniche two-door saloon was dropped.

The new cars were based on the Silver Shadow II base unit, using the same engine and drive train, but with revised rear suspension and mineral oil hydraulics first seen from March 1979 on the coachbuilt Corniche and Camargue.

The objectives that were kept in mind in designing the Silver Spirit range of cars fell into two categories, viz (a) appearance and (b) technical. The new saloon coachwork, with its modern, more angular styling incorporating a lower waistline and

The Silver Spirit saloon as introduced. The radiator shell is 1 inch (25 mm) lower and 3.6 inches (93 mm) wider than that of the Silver Shadow II, and this formerly sharp-edged structure now has slightly radiused edges as a concession to safety.

The Bentley Mulsanne was a Bentley radiatored and badged variant of the Silver Spirit. For the first time the Rolls-Royce and Bentley versions shared a common bonnet lid, its shape and that of the radiator shell having been carefully designed to avoid the need for separate pressings. No radiator mascots were fitted, though one was available as an accessory. This item came with a warning that fitting it to the car would contravene type approval regulations and was the owner's responsibility.

The long wheelbase model in the Silver Spirit range was the Silver Spur. Recognition features, in addition to the extra 4 inches (10 cm) length aft of the centre pillar, included Camargue/Corniche-pattern wheel trims, Silver Spur badging on the boot lid and normally, though not always, an Everflex-covered roof.

The fascia and controls standardised for the Silver Spirit range were, at first, very similar to those of the Silver Shadow II range except that a digital display for time of day, elapsed journey time and outside temperature, as fitted to the Corniche from a year or so earlier, replaced the earlier models' analogue clock and outside temperature gauge. The parking brake was the American-style foot-applied, hand-released type for all markets.

The seating was still in the familiar pleated-and-bolstered style. For the first time in a standard saloon the rear seating consisted of two separate seats that were near duplicates of the front seats. Note the solid black walnut door cappings fitted to these early Silver Spirit range cars. Folding picnic tables in the backs of the front seats, which disappeared from Silver Shadows with a rush of safety consciousness in 1969, became available again, either leather-covered on their outer faces or all polished wood depending on the design requirements of the destination country.

one third greater glass area than its predecessor, has a more eye-catching 'presence' and looks appreciably larger, being in fact 3 inches longer and a little over 2 inches wider. In order to accentuate width, the accent is on the horizontal design features. For the first time Rolls-Royce plumped for large rectangular headlamp units (smaller paired ones for US exports) and large wrap-around rear light clusters, extending on to the boot lid.

The familiar Rolls-Royce radiator shape was, of course, retained, though in a wider, squatter form than that of the earlier cars and rather like that of the Camargue, but with rounded edges for safety reasons. Problems posed by certain countries' legislation regarding bonnet mascots were overcome by the development of an ingeniously designed retracting Spirit of Ecstasy, which withdraws into the radiator shell if struck. Having done so it can be pulled back into position against spring pressure until it latches into place. This version of the mascot dispenses for the first time with the dummy filler cap on which she has been mounted since the filler cap really was a filler cap. For countries with less rigorous mascot laws, the Spirit of Ecstasy remained as she was – spring-mounted on a dummy filler cap with an anti-tamper alarm switch wired to the car's horns. Nowadays the safety mascot is standard for all markets except North America – oddly enough, the country where safety rules are for the most part particularly stringent.

The principal technical objectives of further improved handling and road-holding with even less intrusion of road noise into the car were met by the revised rear suspension arrangement which, like the mineral oil hydraulics, had been quietly introduced on the Corniche and Camargue some 18 months earlier. Compliant front suspension had been introduced on the Silver Shadow in 1972 and rack-and-pinion steering and further front suspension changes on the Silver Shadow II of 1977, so the new rear suspension enabled the rear to catch up, technologically, with

the front. The new design retained the semi-trailing arms of the previous layout, but the pivots are more inclined in order to induce a more pronounced change of camber as the wheels rise and fall. Also, the wheels remain more upright as the car rolls, and consequently it rolls less, giving the tyres more cornering power, improving handling and reducing tyre wear. The levelling rams of the earlier rear suspension were replaced by a Girling self-levelling system that uses each of the rear dampers as a strut, by connecting them via columns of hydraulic fluid (actually mineral oil) to gas springs. The levelling valves adjust the level of oil in the dampers to keep the car's attitude constant regardless of load or load distribution. The car is still suspended on coil springs, but these refinements allow the use of much smaller rear springs, which do not intrude into the boot, and the Girling gas struts are mounted aft of the springs rather than concentric with them as the earlier dampers and levelling rams had been.

A major change that accompanied the incorporation of the new rear suspension layout, firstly on the coachbuilt Corniche and Camargue and subsequently on the Silver Spirit range, was the adoption of Hydraulic Systems Mineral Oil for the hydraulic system in place of RR363, the brake fluid previously employed. As its name implies, HSMO is derived from mineral (i.e. petroleum) sources as opposed to the vegetable by-products and synthetic substances used in the manufacture of conventional brake fluids. The practically universal use by other manufacturers of brake fluids of the conventional type is attributable solely to the fact that the seals in automotive braking systems were originally of natural rubber, which deteriorated rapidly if exposed to mineral oils. In other industries – aviation, machine tools, etc. – mineral oils have been used for many years because compatible materials had been developed for seals in these applications. Now these improved seals, made from synthetic rubbers and plastics, have been adopted in the motor industry – at least by Rolls-Royce.

The benefits inherent in the use of HSMO for motor car hydraulic systems are many. It is much less corrosive and does not have the notoriously effective paint stripping properties of brake fluid when accidentally (or deliberately) spilt on to bodywork. It is non-hydroscopic – i.e. it does not absorb water, thus eliminating the risk of internal corrosion. In the levelling system its superior vibration damping qualities improve ride and noise suppression. Last, but not least, HSMO is a superior lubricant to conventional brake fluid, which has the effect of reducing friction in the braking and levelling systems, thereby prolonging component life.

These advantages bring with them one very real and serious risk – that of contamination of the hydraulic system with brake fluid, and indeed of the inadvertent introduction of mineral oil into an earlier car with a system designed for conventional brake fluid. Either way it is very expensive and potentially dangerous. The smallest amount of the incorrect fluid will eventually ruin all the seals in the system. Naturally, everyone within the Company and the Dealer Network who is directly or indirectly concerned with hydraulic systems is totally aware of the vital importance of using the correct fluid when topping up or carrying out hydraulic system fluid changes. Owners are warned by means of prominent multi-lingual labels on fluid reservoirs of HSMO cars as well as by clear instructions in the car handbook. More recently, lead seals have been fitted to the reservoir filler caps as an additional precaution.

Over the previous five years or so, interest in the Bentley marque had fallen to around a derisory 3 per cent of total car production. With a view to rescuing the marque from oblivion, the opportunity was taken to give the Silver Spirit's Bentley counterpart a distinctive model name – Mulsanne. From this modest beginning the Bentley has never looked back, each successive new Bentley model giving the marque a further shot in the arm. The advent of the Mulsanne Turbo in

The Mulsanne Turbo made its debut at the Geneva Motor Show in March 1982. Such motoring press headlines as 'The Return of the Blower Bentley' and the like made plain the motoring world's astonishment and pleasure at the unexpected appearance of such an exciting new Bentley. Turbo recognition features included a radiator shell painted in the body colour rather than chrome-plated, discrete 'TURBO' badging on the front wings and boot lid, and twin exhaust pipes emerging together on the right-hand side.

Before unleashing a turbocharged car on purchasers with such very high expectations as the customary clientele of Rolls-Royce Motors, the Company had to overcome a number of problems normally associated with turbocharging that would otherwise have rendered the entire concept unacceptable – in particular poor throttle response due to 'turbo lag'. The resultant engine package was dauntingly complex, which explains why Mulsanne Turbos were at first largely confined to the home market where they could be kept under observation. The Garrett AiResearch turbocharger is visible behind its heat-shield on the right and, in the centre, the large cast aluminium air-box, or plenum chamber, which housed the Solex 4A1 four-barrel downdraught carburetter. It is indicative of the rugged nature of Rolls-Royce machinery that few modifications were necessary to render the V-8 fit for the considerable additional stresses resulting from turbocharging. The only significant changes were strengthened pistons and an oil cooler to cope with the higher operating temperature.

1982, later evolving into the superb, ultra-high-performance Turbo R, swept the marque to new heights, ultimately exceeding 50 per cent of total production. Today such magnificent models as the Continental R and Azure keep the Bentley name at the very forefront.

The Bentley Eight was conceived as part of a strategy to build on the success of the Mulsanne Turbo and widen the appeal of the Bentley car to more fully exploit one of the greatest and most famous marques in the annals of motoring. Basically, the Eight as introduced in July 1984 was a standard Mulsanne with stiffened front suspension to enhance the car's

sporting characteristics, slightly reduced interior trim and, as its main external distinguishing feature, a handsome chrome wire mesh radiator grille reminiscent of the famous Bentley Le Mans winners of the 'twenties. It was carefully priced below £50,000 at £49,497, some £5,743 less than the Mulsanne and £12,246 less than the Mulsanne Turbo, in order to attract the new customers that Company research showed would be attracted to Bentley driving with sporting performance and handling and traditional quality standards without the need for full Rolls-Royce luxury specification.

The Bentley Turbo R was

announced in Geneva in March 1985 and provided a decisive answer to criticisms that the Mulsanne Turbo's suspension was too soft for its 135 mph (217 kmph) performance. Roadholding (denoted by the 'R') and handling were dramatically improved by increased anti-roll bar stiffness, slightly stiffened dampers, improved rear subframe sideways location by means of its own hard-rate rubber, bushed Panhard rod, changes to the self-levelling and slightly heavier steering. The Mulsanne Turbo was dropped from the range soon after the introduction of the Turbo R.

In August 1985 Rolls-Royce Motors announced its 100,000th car, a

The Bentley Eight, introduced in mid-1984. At just under £50,000 the Eight was intended to be the lowest priced car in the Rolls-Royce range in order to bring Bentley ownership within range of many more potential new customers, who might not otherwise have considered a Rolls-Royce or Bentley motor car, to build on the revival of interest in the marque created by the Turbo. The external appearance of the Eight represented a further variation on the standard Mulsanne, with a chrome wire mesh grille reminiscent of the famous race-bred Bentleys of the 1920s. The interior furnishings, though slightly reduced in detail, were nevertheless of an extremely high order. The fascia, in straight-grained walnut, was a departure from the more traditional burr walnut veneer. An analogue clock and outside temperature gauge were fitted in lieu of the digital display common to the other saloon models at that time.

As part of the overall strategy to promote a resurgence of interest in the Bentley marque, the Bentley Corniche was marketed from August 1984 as the Continental – a shrewd revival of the evocative name applied to sporting Bentleys from 1952 to early 1966. Recognition features included colour-keyed bumpers, side mirrors and radiator grille vanes.

The Camargue was retained in the Silver Spirit model range until 1986, when it was discontinued. Aside from the adoption of the Silver Spirit technical specification, most components of which it received along with the Corniche some 18 months before the introduction of the Silver Spirit range, the Camargue remained aloof and visually uninfluenced by the new models. It was discontinued in 1986 after a small final run of Limited Edition cars.

The Bentley Turbo R. Cast alloy wheels with Pirelli's safety rims carrying Pirelli low-profile (275/55VR15) tyres lent this model a distinctive external appearance. A special fascia was introduced, with comprehensive instrumentation, including a revolution counter alongside the speedometer, and a full console between the front seats.

The 100,000th Rolls-Royce car – actually the combined total of Rolls-Royce and post-1931 Bentley motor cars made by Rolls-Royce – was a commemorative 'Centenary' version of the Silver Spur. The photograph shows the Silver Spur Centenary car with, behind, some of a select Limited Edition of 12 replicas for the USA, eight for the home market and five for Europe and the Middle East – all eagerly snapped up! The original Silver Spur Centenary is now in the custody of the Rolls-Royce Enthusiasts' Club.

1986 model year Bentleys benefited from the fitting of a handsome variant of the distinctive alloy wheels of the Turbo R. These were standard for the Continental and the Mulsanne, and available as an extra cost option for the Eight (pictured).

The 1987 model year Corniche was redesignated 'Corniche II' for the US market only. This designation was extended to other markets from the following year. Advantage was taken of the 14 per cent increase in power output from the fuel-injected engine over the previous four-barrel Solex installation to raise the final drive ratio to 2.69:1 for even more effortless high-speed cruising.

In October 1987 the Bentley Mulsanne S was introduced. This model featured the Turbo R style of centre console and instrumentation to give the Mulsanne a more distinctly sporting character. Straight-grain walnut interior woodwork was specified for this model, though burr walnut was available at extra cost. The Mulsanne S was successfully launched in the United States, where it was the first Bentley model available for more than a decade.

1989 model year Bentley saloons were further distinguished from their Rolls-Royce counterparts by a purposeful new frontal appearance with paired 7-inch round headlights for all markets, colour-keyed door mirrors and bright cantrail finishers. Pictured is the 1989 Bentley Eight.

For the 1990 model year the changes were considered sufficient to warrant a change of model names to Silver Spirit II, Silver Spur II and Corniche III. This is the Silver Spirit II, the main external distinguishing feature of which was the new alloy wheels with polished stainless trims.

The 1990 Silver Spirit II and Silver Spur II interior featured an inlaid and crossbanded burr walnut fascia. The new gear range selector indicator can just be seen in the warning light panel, while more obvious are the new leather-covered steering wheel, two additional air conditioning outlets at the extremities of the fascia and the ignition/lighting switchbox of revised design at the right of the leather-covered knee-roll. The centre console included switches for seat heaters.

The 1990 Bentley saloons shared the new technical features of their Rolls-Royce counterparts but retained their own distinctive alloy wheel designs and did not receive the series II tag. The fascia layout changes also applied to the Bentleys, but not the new inlaid woodwork style.

In order to allow the Company to continue to offer a large, spacious limousine once the Phantom VI had been discontinued, a new limousine version of the Silver Spur was developed by Mulliner Park Ward in London. At first this was to be called the 'Mulliner Park Ward Silver Spur II Limousine', but following the virtual closure of Mulliner Park Ward's London operations, construction of this model was transferred to Crewe and the name Rolls-Royce Touring Limousine was adopted.

Both the new inlaid woodwork and the leather-covered steering wheel (for the US market this was different and incorporated an air bag restraint system) were applied to the revised version of the Corniche, called Corniche III.

On 5 March 1991, at the Geneva Motor Show, the Bentley Continental R was launched, for deliveries commencing in the 1992 model year. With no front quarter-lights the traditional stainless steel door window frames would not have been sufficiently stiff for good sealing at the speeds of which the car is capable, so the doors are one-piece steel structures with heavy window frames extending into the roof; slim stainless steel finishers preserve the traditional appearance.

For 1992 the Corniche acquired the Automatic Ride Control that had been fitted to the saloon models since 1990, together with a new hood with heated glass rear window, becoming Corniche IV in the process. The Bentley Continental convertible acquired the same specification changes but remained unchanged in name.

The 1993 Bentley Brooklands saloon at speed on the famous banked Brooklands track near Byfleet, Surrey – the birthplace of British motor racing after which this Bentley was named. Note the radiator shell finished in the body colour and the absence of a chrome moulding along the bonnet centre-line.

The 1994 Silver Spirit III and long-wheelbase Silver Spur III (pictured) saloons remained virtually unchanged in external appearance – save for the badges on the boot lid – from their predecessors the Silver Spirit II and Silver Spur II. However, interior and, particularly, technical changes were significant, and the Silver Spirit III shared the painted trim rings on the wheel covers with its long-wheelbase counterpart.

This view of the revised facia of the Silver Spirit III and Silver Spur III provides a glimpse of the new seats. The driver's air bag is contained within the steering wheel while the passenger side air bag is installed in the area previously occupied by the glove compartment and is concealed behind a veneered, hinged flap; a new lockable stowage space was provided under the fascia. Bentley models retained their more sporting and more comprehensively instrumented fascia, while incorporating all the new features.

The Bentley models retained their existing model designations and remained unchanged in external appearance in all but detail. The Turbo R (pictured) gained subtly re-styled 16-inch wheels and lost its chrome bonnet divider strip, thus becoming even more difficult to distinguish from the naturally aspirated Brooklands.

The Bentley Continental R acquired completely re-styled 17-inch wheels for 1994. Both this model and the Turbo R benefited from new Electronic Transient Boost Control, which temporarily overrides the turbocharger's normal maximum boost when full acceleration is called for, such as when overtaking.

commemorative 'Centenary' version of the Silver Spur, in Royal Blue. At a special hand-over ceremony at Crewe, the two longest-serving employees, Mrs Margaret Green, 58, and Mr Jack Goodwin, 62, officially presented Chief Executive Richard Perry with the car's keys and registration documents for the Company's safe keeping. The name Silver Spur Centenary paid tribute to Britain's 1985 national celebration of a century of motoring.

For the 1990 model year the Silver Spirit became the Silver Spirit II, with a host of new and innovative technical improvements such as Adaptive Ride Control. Anti-lock braking (ABS) had been introduced in 1987.

In March 1991 Rolls-Royce Motor Cars Ltd launched the Bentley Continental R. As a sleek and stylish two-door car it fills a space in the range left by the 1986 departure of the Camargue.

With the resurgent interest in the Bentley marque from the early 1980s came thoughts of an exclusive Bentley body style, and Peter Ward, then Chief Executive, is known to have favoured this approach to the marque's future. Public response to the 1985 'Project 90', a full-size glass-fibre mock-up Bentley coupé exhibited at the 1985 Geneva Motor Show, left no doubt about the strength of appeal of such an individual Bentley, and the decision to proceed with an exclusive Bentley model that

would further enhance the marque's sporting image was taken.

After considering – and rejecting – the idea of a two-door version of the standard saloon, a dedicated body style, designed with the aid of John Heffernan and Ken Greenley of International Automotive Design, was settled on. Radical departures from tradition were incorporated into the design, including cut-into-roof doors and sophisticated use of new composite materials for the integrated bumper system. The traditional skills of the coachbuilder were complimented by the latest computer technology to create a shape appropriate to the marque, of distinctive appearance and with good high-speed stability and low wind noise.

Rolls-Royce and Bentley owners have become accustomed to the sight of a bewildering array of plumbing, trunking, wiring and electronic equipment largely obscuring the view of the engine when they open their bonnets. For 1994 the under-bonnet view was improved by the fitting of a new engine cover featuring a machined aluminium cooling grille. Additional covers are fitted to the inner wing valances on all but the convertible models. New heads and manifolding allowed the 6.75-litre V-8 engine to deliver 20 per cent more power with improved fuel economy and cleaner emissions.

During 1994 Rolls-Royce Motor Cars Ltd announced two 'niche' models – the Rolls-Royce Flying Spur and the Bentley Turbo S. The Flying Spur borrowed both its name and engine from Bentley models – the name from a famous Bentley Continental of the 1950s and '60s and the engine from the Bentley Turbo models. The Bentley Turbo S anticipated the 1996 model year cars with its even more powerful engine, higher, integrated bumpers and resultant lower grille shell. The 17-inch alloy wheels were the same as those of the 1994 model year Continental R. Such 'niche' models enabled the Company to keep sales up during the difficult years from 1991 to 1994.

As had been the case with the original Bentley Continental 40 years before, the Continental R body shape was wind-tunnel proven, the well-contoured form and carefully raked windscreen proving their worth with notably lower Cd (drag coefficient) than the current cars. This also brings benefits in reduced fuel consumption and enhanced performance. It is worth recording that when the Continental R was unveiled at Geneva it was one of the few occasions on which the assembled throng has broken into a spontaneous round of applause at the first sight of a new car.

The Continental R interior styling is reassuringly familiar, with similar seating to that of the Turbo R and a basically similar layout to the instruments and controls, except that the centre console extends into the rear compartment. The electric gear range selector is mounted in the centre console – the first time that this had been anywhere other than on the steering column on an automatic Bentley. The automatic transmission itself is also new, having four forward speeds with the direct drive in third and an overdrive fourth speed for even more effortless low-rpm cruising and improved fuel economy. (For the 1992 model year this new automatic gearbox was standardised for all Rolls-Royce and Bentley models.)

The Continental R is fitted with the turbocharged engine of the Turbo R,

providing scorching performance. Top speed of the current version is 155 mph (250 kmph) and acceleration from 0 to 60 mph takes under 6 seconds. A very fast flying B, taking the Bentley marque into a challenging new era.

In August 1993 a further significant revision of the Rolls-Royce and Bentley model range was announced. The standard and long wheelbase Rolls-Royce saloons became the Silver Spirit III and Silver Spur III respectively, all other model designations remaining unchanged.

More than 70 engineering changes were made, requiring the greatest ever investment by the Company in the improvement of an existing model range. At the heart of the package of improvements was a new version of the 6.75-litre V-8 engine, which blended state-of-the-art technology with a proven layout to create an engine that produced dramatically more power across the speed range, providing the Rolls-Royce four-door saloons with a top speed well in excess of 130 mph (210 kmph), while improving refinement still further. Redesigned cylinder heads and manifolding were largely responsible for the increased power output.

To further improve occupant safety and comfort, air bags were introduced as standard for both driver and front seat passenger.

The responsiveness and performance of the Bentley Turbo R and Continental R models, which

were already remarkable by any standards, were further improved by the development of Electronic Transient Boost Control. This temporarily overrides the turbocharger's normal maximum boost when full load acceleration is required, effectively over-boosting the engine during the initial stages of heavy acceleration, such as when overtaking.

On 7 March 1995, at the Geneva Motor Show, Rolls-Royce Motor Cars Ltd unveiled a convertible version of the Continental R, which it called the Bentley Azure. This is the first entirely new convertible since 1967. The much acclaimed Continental R lines were superbly adapted to convertible form with the assistance of Pininfarina of Italy, arguably the world leaders in convertible styling. Chris Woodwark, the then newly appointed Chief Executive of Rolls-Royce Motor Cars Ltd (replacing Peter Ward), was delighted with this first new model following his appointment: 'We have shown how we continue to develop new models that exceed the highest expectations of our customers and set new standards at the peak of the performance and luxury car market. Great credit is due to the Bentley design team at Crewe and our colleagues at Pininfarina. We believe this to be the most exciting product announcement in recent years. It represents another major step forward for this company, and one in which

Mr Chris Woodwark, BSc (Econ), DipM, FCIM, Chief Executive, Rolls-Royce Motor Cars Ltd.

we can all take great pride'. Mr Woodwark is also Chairman of fellow Vickers Group company Cosworth Engineering and Executive Director of the parent company, Vickers PLC.

For the 1996 model year cars, unveiled at the RREC Annual Rally in June 1995, the numerical suffix was dropped entirely, which means that the Rolls-Royce models are once again the Silver Spirit and Silver Spur. They are significantly revised new versions of the existing Silver Spirit range of cars. The new Bentley range comprises the Brooklands, Turbo R, Continental R and Azure. Both the Brooklands and the Turbo R may be ordered in long wheelbase form.

The changes embodied in these new cars are quite notable, in both the visual and technical areas, and bring significant economy and refinement gains. In fact, a £25 million development programme has made the new cars the most technically advanced, refined and fuel-efficient in the Company's history, and ensures that Rolls-Royce and Bentley motor cars remain at the very pinnacle of the automotive pyramid.

The four-door saloon models are changed as follows:

- New, higher-mounted bumpers integrated with the front spoiler and rear valance;
- Front quarter-lights deleted to make way for a new side-window-mounted exterior mirror system;
- The spare wheel is now located in a well below the floor of the luggage compartment rather than in a swing-down cradle as before. This gives the rear of the car a cleaner line below the higher rear bumper;
- The radiator shell is reduced in height to suit the higher front bumper. On Rolls-Royce models the mascot is reduced in size by around 20 per cent to blend better with the lowered grille;
- New 16-inch wheels for the Rolls-Royce models. The Bentley Brooklands wheels are also now 16 inches and of an entirely new design, while the Turbo R receives the 17-inch wheels of the previous Continental R, and the new Continental R shares the wheel design previously seen on the Azure.
- A new fascia and centre console design is shared by all the saloon models, with detail differences between Rolls-Royce and Bentley models in style of woodwork, instrumentation and centre console shape and layout;
- An electrically adjustable steering wheel provides easier access in and out of the driver's seat and, with the new mirrors, is incorporated into the seat memory positions;
- Dedicated air conditioning controls in a new console for rear seat passengers.
- New cylinder heads, throttle body, low-loss intake system, higher final drive ratio and a new engine management system provide a 12 per cent improvement in fuel economy, along with a modest 1 per cent improvement in performance on the naturally aspirated Silver Spirit, Silver Spur and Bentley Brooklands. The turbocharged Bentley Turbo R, Continental R and Azure benefit to the tune of 7 per cent in economy and 8 per cent in performance, due to the addition of a liquid-cooled charge-cooler and a Zytek engine management system.

Chief Executive Chris Woodwark commented: 'The far-reaching improvements made by the project team are sufficient for many manufacturers to call these "new" models. Of course, we will not rest here but continue to find new ways to ensure our customers can experience the ultimate in luxury motoring.'

What of the future for the Rolls-Royce and Bentley motor car? The Bentley Concept Java, unveiled at the Geneva Motor Show in March 1994, perhaps provides a glimpse of what the future holds. For some years the Company has been moving towards a divergence of the Rolls-Royce and Bentley marques, and it seems that the 'badge engineering' that began to creep in soon after the end of the Second World War may become a thing of the past. Already, the two marques seem uncomfortable sharing the same body shell for the four-door saloons, and the current cars will almost certainly be the last to which that situation applies.

The proposed specification announced for Concept Java included a 3.5-litre, twin overhead camshaft, 32-valve, twin turbo V-8 engine conceived in conjunction with fellow Vickers Group company Cosworth Engineering. However, at the end of 1994, following much media speculation, Rolls-Royce Motor Cars Ltd signed a technical collaboration agreement with BMW to develop Concept Java and new engines for future Rolls-Royce and Bentley cars. Future Rolls-Royce models will have a 5.4-litre V-12 and Bentleys will have a 4.4-litre turbocharged V-8, both developed under the technical collaboration agreement and probably at least partially of BMW manufacture. It is believed that the Bentley engine will receive the 'full Cosworth treatment'. If this is a little disappointing in view of the fact that Rolls-Royce has always been famed for its engines, it must be remembered that the car maker is no longer part of the large aero engine company. With annual production of 3,000 cars in an exceptionally good year and currently around half that, it would be beyond the resources of Rolls-Royce Motor

The Bentley Concept Java, a concept model with possible future production in mind, was unveiled at the Geneva Motor Show in March 1994. With its carbon fibre coupé roof attached, Concept Java showed a close family resemblance to the larger Continental R.

The Bentley Continental T, introduced in June 1996, is based on the Continental R, though its styling, engineering and appointments are designed to more dramatically reflect the thoroughbred attributes of the Bentley marque. Power output of the 6,750 cc turbocharged V-8 engine is nearly 400 bhp, with more than 590 lb/ft of torque. 18 inch wheels and wheelbase shortened by some 4 inches give the Continental T an even more distinctive, sporting stance.

The interior design of the Continental T reflects the dynamic exterior, with a hand-worked 'engine turned' aluminium fascia and straight grain mahogany waistrails. New sports seats and extraordinarily comprehensive instrumentation with chrome bezel instrument surrounds add to the effect.

Cars Ltd to develop an entirely new engine on its own.

On the other hand, the money saved by the BMW deal, said to be around £45 million, is being used to build a new body facility at Crewe to make Rolls-Royce independent of Pressed Steel Fisher in Oxford, who have supplied all the four-door saloon body shells from the earliest Bentley Mk VI standard steel saloons. Ironically, PSF is now owned by Rover, in turn owned nowadays by

BMW! The Company is therefore about to become independent of BMW for bodies, but dependant upon the same manufacturer for engines!

Future Rolls-Royce and Bentley saloon models will be based on a common body frame but panelled differently for each marque, to give each a distinct and separate identity. Re-skinning of BMW designs has not been considered and there is no question of any BMW take-over of, or even equity in, Rolls-Royce Motor

Cars. In fact, much has been said and written about the alleged vulnerability of Rolls-Royce Motor Cars Ltd to foreign take-over, but being a part of the financially secure Vickers group of companies means that the risk of such an eventuality is at least minimised, while the Vickers management has unequivocally stated that the Company is not for sale. Its future within the present ownership, building the best motor cars in the world, appears secure.

The latest limousine from Crewe is the Rolls-Royce Park Ward, the marque's flagship model. No more than 20 of this model will be built each year.

Rolls-Royce Park Ward are able to create their own interior specification by choosing from a palette which may include television and video, personalised hide and veneers, rear seat bureau . . . allowing unlimited scope for individualisation.

Hand machining the 'engine turned' aluminium fascia for the Bentley Continental T.

TECHNICAL SPECIFICATIONS

Silver Spirit and derivative models, 1980 to present

Engine

Eight cylinders in 90-degree vee formation, aluminium alloy block with cast iron wet cylinder liners and aluminium cylinder heads.
Bore 4.1 inches (104.1 mm), stroke 3.9 inches (99.1 mm), cubic capacity 412 cu in (6,750 cc). Overhead valves worked by gear-driven camshaft in vee of engine. Five-bearing crankshaft. Two SU type HIF.7 (1⅞ inch) carburetters.

1989: Cross-bolted crankcase.
Cars for North America and Japan: Bosch K-Jetronic continuous fuel injection system with 'closed loop' mixture control.
Bentley Mulsanne Turbo and Turbo R: Solex type 4A1 four-barrel downdraught with partial throttle fuel economy device.
From 1987 model year, all models, all markets: Fuel injection standard.
From 1989 model year: MK Motronic fuel injection and engine management system.
From 1996 model year Bentley turbocharged models: Zytek EMS3 engine management system.

Chassis

Monocoque construction with separate front and rear sub-frames:
Front – steel box-section construction mounted to car underframe by rubber mounts.
Rear – comprises rear suspension and final drive cross-members connected by tubular members to form rigid structure. Attached to car underframe by cylindrical rubber mounts. Short telescopic damper fitted to each front mount to dampen fore and aft movement.

Dimensions

Overall length 17 ft 3.42 in (5,268 mm) plus 4 in (100 mm) (long wheelbase cars).
Wheelbase 10 ft 0.5 in (3,061 mm) (standard), 10 ft 4.5 in (3,162 mm) (long wheelbase).
Front track 5 ft 1 in (1,549 mm).
Rear track 5 ft 1 in (1,549 mm).
Kerbside weight of car, between 4,950 lb (2,245 kg) and 5,340 lb (2,420 kg), depending on body type and country of domicile.

Transmission

At introduction: General Motors type GM400 three-speed torque converter automatic transmission.
Bentley Continental R and all models from 1992 model year: General Motors four-speed torque converter automatic transmission with overdrive top gear, electronically linked to engine management system.
All cars have electrically operated gear selection with control mounted on right side of steering column (except Bentley Continental R, Bentley Brooklands and four-speed Bentley Turbo R and Bentley Azure, which have centre-console-mounted gear selector).
Propeller shaft: dynamically balanced, single straight tube with rubber jointed coupling at front and rear.
Final drive ratio *at introduction* 3.08:1 *(Bentley Mulsanne Turbo, Turbo R, Continental R and all models from 1992 model year, 2.69:1).*

Steering

Power-assisted rack-and-pinion with centre take-off. Power assistance by hydraulic pressure from Saginaw engine-driven pump. Energy-absorbing collapsible steering column. Turns, lock-to-lock, 3.25.

1996 model year cars: Electrically tilting steering wheel.

Suspension

Front: independent by coil springs with lower wishbones, compliant controlled upper levers, telescopic

dampers and anti-roll bar mounted on front sub-frame.
Rear: independent by coil springs with semi-trailing arms, gas springs in conjunction with suspension struts acting as integral dampers and height control rams. Anti-roll bar.

From 1990 model year, Silver Spirit II and derivatives (except Corniche III): Electronic three-position automatic ride control system.
From 1992 model year, Corniche IV: Electronic three-position automatic ride control system.

Hydraulic system

Two camshaft-driven hydraulic pumps delivering Hydraulic Systems Mineral Oil under pressure (up to 2,500 psi) to pair of hydraulic accumulators mounted on either side of crankcase. Hydraulic pressure stored in accumulators is used for braking and height control systems. Two low-pressure warning lights on fascia, one for each hydraulic circuit.

Height control system

Fully automatic hydraulic height control system to maintain standing height of car under all load conditions, by means of height control rams integral with rear gas springs. System operates at two speeds – slow levelling when driving and fast levelling with the gear selector lever in neutral or park.

Brakes

11-inch disc brakes on all four wheels. Each front wheel fitted with two twin-cylinder callipers and each rear wheel with one four-cylinder calliper. Two separate and independent hydraulic circuits from the high-pressure hydraulic system operated by distribution valves connected to brake pedal. Foot-applied, hand-release parking brake. Separate brake pads for parking brake.

1989 model year cars: Anti-lock brakes (ABS).

Exhaust system

Cars not fitted with catalytic converter: Twin pipe system with six silencer boxes.
Cars fitted with catalytic converter: Twin downtake pipes from engine merge into single pipe prior to catalytic converter, after which system reverts to dual system with twin intermediate and rear silencer boxes.

Road wheels and tyres

At introduction: 15-inch pressed steel wheels with 235/70 HR15 steel braced radial ply tyres.
Bentley Turbo R: 15-inch aluminium alloy wheels with 265/65 R15 low-profile radial ply tyres.
Other Bentley models from 1986 (optional at first on Eight): 15-inch aluminium alloy wheels.
Silver Spirit II, Silver Spur II, Corniche III, Corniche IV: 15-inch aluminium alloy wheels with stainless steel covers.
Bentley Continental R: 16-inch aluminium alloy wheels with 255/60 ZR16 low-profile radial ply tyres.
1994 model year Bentley Turbo R: 16-inch aluminium alloy wheels with 255/60 ZR16 low-profile radial ply tyres.
1994 model year Bentley Continental R: 17-inch aluminium alloy wheels with 255/55 ZR17 low-profile radial ply tyres.
1996 model year Silver Spirit, Silver Spur, Bentley Brooklands: 16-inch aluminium alloy wheels with 235/65VR16 tyres.
1996 model year Bentley Turbo R, Bentley Azure: 17-inch aluminium alloy wheels with 255/55WR17 directional tyres.

Coachwork

Saloon models: Four-door monocoque construction pressed steel saloon with aluminium doors, bonnet and boot. long wheelbase saloon of similar construction.
Corniche and Bentley Continental convertibles: Welded steel construction by Mulliner Park Ward on suitably reinforced base unit, with aluminium doors, bonnet and boot.
Limousine: Silver Spur body specially extended and finished by Mulliner Park Ward.

CHASSIS NUMBERS (Vehicle Identification Number)

Silver Spirit

Includes all derivative models and the Phantom VI from 1980.

In October 1980, when the Silver Spirit range of cars was introduced, an entirely new system of numbering was adopted. This was the 17-digit Vehicle Identification Number (VIN), an American device adopted by the International Standards Organisation for world use. Each of the first 12 digits has a specific meaning, detailed below. The remaining five digits made up the car's number. The sample VIN below is that of the first production Silver Spirit, followed by an explanation of the meaning of the 17 digits. It should be noted that the VIN was also adopted for models carried over from the previous range, i.e. Corniche, Camargue and Phantom VI.

S	C	A	Z	S	0	0	0	0	A	C	H	0	1	0	0	1
1	2	3	4	5	6	7	8	9	10	11	12	13	14	15	16	17

1 and 2 = World Manufacturer
    Identifier (country)
    S – Europe
    C – England

3 = World Manufacturer Identifier
    (marque)
    A – Rolls-Royce
    B – Bentley

4 = chassis or underframe type
    P – Phantom VI
    Y – Camargue and early
        Corniche VINs
    Z – all other models

5 = body type
    S – saloon
    L – long wheelbase with division

N – long wheelbase, no division
D – Convertible
J – Camargue
M – Phantom VI Limousine
T – Phantom VI Landaulette

From the 1987 model year, L and T were dropped and the following new body type digits were phased in:

E – Bentley Eight* (1988 other than America)
F – Bentley Eight L (1988 other than America)
R – Bentley Turbo R (from 1989 model year)
P – Bentley Turbo RL (from 1989 model year)
X – Silver Spur and Mulsanne L Limousine
W – Silver Spur II Touring Limousine (1992)
B – Bentley Continental R (1992)
N – Long Wheelbase (with or without division)
M – Phantom VI (all body types)
K – Bentley Azure (1995 onwards)
*E – Bentley Brooklands from 1993 model year

6 = US requirement – indicates engine type.

Cars for all other markets initially had 0000 for the unused digits 6 to 9. Later, these digits came into use for all markets.

4 – type L410 engine
8 – Bentley Eight
0 – other than America

7 = carburetters or fuel injection
1 – carburetters

2 – fuel injection
T – Turbo
0 – other than America

From the 1987 model year the following engine type codes were phased in for digits 6 and 7:

00 – naturally aspirated, fuel injected
01 – naturally aspirated, carburetters (Phantom VI only)
02 – naturally aspirated, fuel injected, catalyst equipped
03 – turbocharged, catalyst equipped
04 – turbocharged

8 = occupant restraint system
A – active belts
B – passive belts – front (USA only)
C – air bags
D – Driver-only air bag, passenger active belts
0 – other than America (prior to 1987 model year)

9 = check digit

A US requirement – used to ensure VIN is correct and to foil would-be VIN forgers. If the VIN is incorrect at any one digit, the check digit will show this. The check digit is 0 to 9 or X.

10 = year

Indicates the model year for which, not necessarily *in* which, a car was built (except in the case of the

Phantom VI, the year letter of which indicates the year in which the chassis was laid down).

A – 1980
B – 1981
C – 1982
D – 1983
E – 1984
F – 1985
G – 1986
H – 1987
J – 1988
K – 1989
L – 1990
M – 1991
N – 1992
P – 1993
R – 1994
S – 1995
T – 1996
V – 1997
W – 1998
X – 1999
Y – 2000

11 = factory
C – Crewe
W – Willesden

Note that this refers to the chassis, not the coachwork. Only the Phantom VI chassis was built at Willesden (Hythe Road) and was thus the only model to have the W digit.

12 = steering position
H – right-hand drive
X – export

13-17 = sequential identification number, commencing with 01001 in 1980

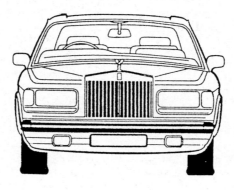

Rolls-Royce chronology, 1904-1996

The following chronology of Rolls-Royce includes a number of significant aero and other records and achievements not related to motor cars until 1971, when the Aero and Car Divisions became separate companies.

1904 April: First complete Royce car test driven.
23 December: Working agreement signed between Royce Ltd and C. S. Rolls & Co. Cars to be called 'Rolls-Royce'.

1905 Royce designed and built one of first V-8 engines.

1906 16 March: Rolls-Royce Ltd registered as a company.
C. S. Rolls won Isle of Man TT in Rolls-Royce 20 hp.
First 40/50 hp chassis exhibited at Olympia Motor Show.

1907 First complete 40/50 hp car exhibited.

1908 9 July: Derby factory opened by Lord Montagu of Beaulieu.

1910 11 July: C. S. Rolls killed at Bournemouth – first Englishman to be killed in an air accident.

1912 London-Edinburgh type 40/50 hp chassis introduced.

1914 Design work started on first Rolls-Royce aero engine – the Eagle.

1919 Record flights in Eagle-powered Vickers Vimy aircraft – first direct flights across Atlantic, to Australia and South Africa.

1922 Twenty Horsepower car introduced.

1925 New Phantom introduced.

1929 Supermarine S.6 seaplane powered by 'R' engine won Schneider Trophy at 328.63 mph. Phantom II and 20/25 cars introduced.

1931 Schneider Trophy won outright by Supermarine S.6B at 407 mph; land speed records in Bluebird, Speed of the Wind and Thunderbolt; water speed records in Miss England II and III, Bluebird II and III – all powered by 'R' engine.
Bentley Motors purchased by Rolls-Royce Ltd.

1933 Bentley 3½ Litre introduced. Death of Sir Henry Royce.

1936 Phantom III, 25/30 and Bentley 4¼ Litre introduced.
First Merlin engine on test.

1938 New Chassis Division formed.
Wraith introduced.
Crewe factory opened for Merlin aero engine production.

1939 Coachbuilding firm Park Ward & Co Ltd acquired by Rolls-Royce Ltd.
Bentley Mk V introduced just as Second World War broke out.
Crewe's first Merlin engines produced.

1943 First Rolls-Royce jet engine, the Welland.

1944 Gloster Meteor, with Rolls-Royce Welland engine – only allied jet aircraft in Second World War.

1945 Rolls-Royce Trent – world's first turbo-prop engine.

1946 Car Division established at Crewe factory.
Production of Rolls-Royce and Bentley cars resumed.
Bentley Mk VI – first car with standard steel saloon coachwork.
Silver Wraith introduced.

1949 Silver Dawn – first Rolls-Royce car with standard steel saloon coachwork.

1950 First Phantom IV delivered.

1951 First transatlantic jet flight without refuelling, by Avon-powered English Electric Canberra. First of many Rolls-Royce Avon records.

1952 Bentley R-type – first automatic gearbox. Bentley Continental introduced.

1955 Silver Cloud and Bentley S-type introduced.

1959 Silver Cloud II, Bentley S2 and Phantom V introduced. Coachbuilding firm H. J. Mulliner & Co Ltd acquired by Rolls-Royce Ltd.

1961 H. J. Mulliner and Park Ward merged to form H. J. Mulliner, Park Ward Ltd.

1962 Silver Cloud III and Bentley S3 introduced.

1965 Silver Shadow and Bentley T Series introduced.

1968 Phantom VI introduced.

1971 New independent motor car company formed – Rolls-Royce Motors Ltd. Corniche introduced.

1975 Camargue introduced. Silver Shadow II and Bentley T2 introduced. Long-wheelbase car called Silver Wraith II.

1980 Rolls-Royce Motors Ltd merged with Vickers. Silver Spirit, Silver Spur and Bentley Mulsanne introduced.

1982 Bentley Mulsanne Turbo introduced.

1983 Company name within Vickers PLC group changed to Rolls-Royce Motor Cars Ltd.

1984 Bentley Eight introduced.

1985 Bentley Turbo R introduced. Bentley Corniche renamed Bentley Continental.

1986 Bentley Mulsanne S introduced.

1989 Silver Spirit II, Silver Spur II introduced for 1990 model year. Bentley saloons shared new specification but model names unchanged.

1991 Bentley Continental R introduced.

1992 Bentley Brooklands replaced Mulsanne S and Eight.

1993 Silver Spirit III and Silver Spur III introduced. Bentley saloons shared new specification but model names unchanged.

1994 Mulliner Park Ward London (Willesden) operations closed. Bentley Concept Java announced. Limited Edition Rolls-Royce Flying Spur, Bentley Turbo S and Continental S introduced.

1995 Bentley Azure introduced. New 1996 model year Silver Spirit and Silver Spur (with numerical appellations dropped) announced at RREC Annual Rally. Bentley saloons shared new specification but model names unchanged.

1996 Bentley Continental T, Bentley Turbo R Sport and Rolls-Royce Park Ward introduced.

Index